Say It With Charts
Workbook

GENE ZELAZNY

Edited by Steve Sakson

McGraw-Hill

New York   Chicago   San Francisco   Lisbon   London
Madrid   Mexico City   Milan   New Delhi   San Juan
Seoul   Singapore   Sydney   Toronto

The McGraw·Hill Companies

3 4 5 6 7 8 9 0   DOC/DOC   0 9 8 7

ISBN 0-07-144162-X

Contents

Say It With Charts
WorkBook

Introduction

In my book *Say It with Charts*, I lay out some easy techniques that business people can use to create visual presentations that are powerful, persuasive, and eye-catching. However, if you're like many who face the challenge of mastering this skill, you know it takes time, patience, and, most of all, practice, practice, and more practice. That's why I offer you this workbook.

In it, you'll find three things:

- A series of business charts that I've gathered from real-life situations

- A challenge to you to improve them

- Suggested improvements to communicate the information more quickly and clearly.

Your challenge in this workbook is to avoid the temptation of simply flipping the page to see my solution. Instead, I encourage you to study the charts and use the space you'll find below them to sketch your ideas for improvement. Then, turn the page to compare your ideas with what I came up with in the real world and what led to my thinking.

As you accept this challenge, understand that I am in no way claiming that my answer is the best one. In fact, I have every confidence that your answer could work just as well. The important thing is that you take a critical look to determine what the level of improvement can be.

Also, understand that there's nothing requiring you to do these exercises sequentially. Start anywhere. Dip in and out. Come back to the same example again as new ideas come up. I hope that after you've done a few of these you'll conclude that "playing it with charts" can actually be fun.

Before you start, let me offer this quick refresher on the fundamentals of charts. As readers of *Say It with Charts* will remember, charts generally fall into two broad categories:

- Data charts, also called quantitative charts, depict numbers graphically to make a point.

- Concept charts, also called nonquantitative charts, use words and images.

Of course, some charts use elements of both categories.

Data Charts

We can translate data into five kinds of comparisons.
Each comparison is shown best by a specific chart form.
Here's a reminder of how they are best used.

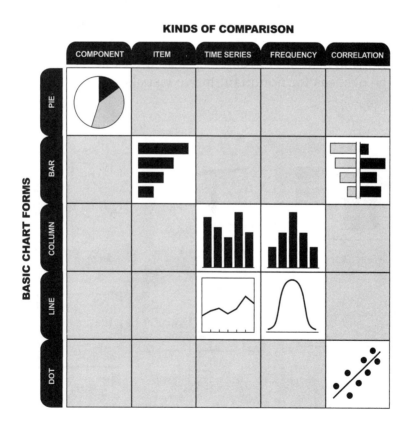

Concept Charts

Concept charts describe a situation, such as interaction, interrelationship, leverage, or forces at work. There are basic examples in the visual below, but for some "thought starters," before you tackle the exercises in this workbook, allow me to turn your attention to the fourth edition of *Say It with Charts*. In Section 3 of the book, you'll find "Solutions in Search of Problems," a chapter that offers a range of ideas for nonquantitative visuals.

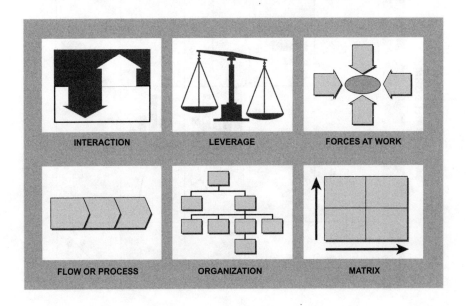

As you begin your journey through this workbook, you'll notice I've presented the examples in a jumbled manner. That's to keep you on your toes. However, to help get you started, here are some broad categories for solutions to both data and concept charts. These solutions are by no means exhaustive. I call them:

- Simpler is better.

- More is better.

- Different is better.

- Creativity is better.

Take a look at the samples of each of these solutions on the following pages.

Simpler is better

In this solution, we remove details from the chart that get in the way of the message we're trying to send. This isn't always easy. It's a natural tendency to want to give your audience as much information as possible.

The problem is that this prompts you to present too much information, so your audience actually absorbs and retains very little of it.

The "simpler is better" solution requires you to think hard about the message you really want to convey in a chart, and eliminate material that distracts from that message.

Here's an example. The top chart supports the point that PVC is the lowest-cost polymer. Here, you're quick to see that it shows all the data gathered during the problem-solving stage to make the point. This might be okay for a paper document, in which readers can spend as much time with the chart as they need. But if you're presenting this chart to an audience, onscreen, the content should be greatly simplified.

For example:

- Do we need two measures of cost performance to support the same message—one expressed in cents per pound, the other in cents per cubic inch? *No. Cents per pound will do.*

- Must we show the data at the end of every bar?
  No. A scale will be sufficient to show the relationships.

In addition to these changes that make the chart simpler, I've changed the sequence of the bars, ranking them from high to low, to better show PVC's position. The new chart with less data focuses attention on the message that PVC's cost is lower than that of all other polymers.

CURRENT COST OF PVC IS COMPETITIVE WITH OTHER MATERIALS

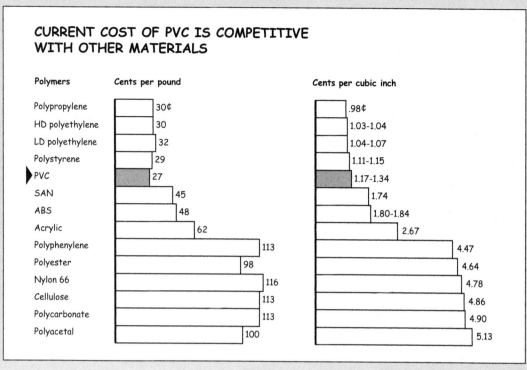

Polymers	Cents per pound	Cents per cubic inch
Polypropylene	30¢	.98¢
HD polyethylene	30	1.03-1.04
LD polyethylene	32	1.04-1.07
Polystyrene	29	1.11-1.15
▶ PVC	27	1.17-1.34
SAN	45	1.74
ABS	48	1.80-1.84
Acrylic	62	2.67
Polyphenylene	113	4.47
Polyester	98	4.64
Nylon 66	116	4.78
Cellulose	113	4.86
Polycarbonate	113	4.90
Polyacetal	100	5.13

PVC—LEAST EXPENSIVE POLYMER

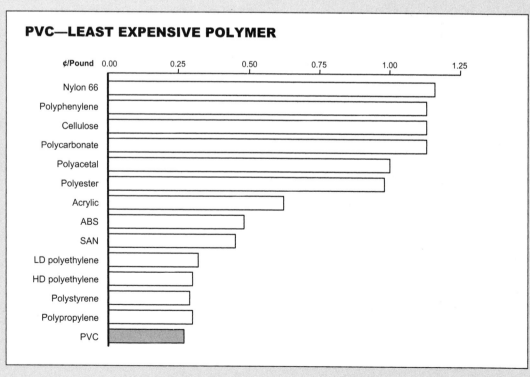

More is better

Here, we create multiple charts to give a message that is too complex to be told on just one chart.

Sometimes, your goal for the presentation requires you to keep the details that you might eliminate if you used a "Simpler is better" solution. So you go back to cramming too much stuff on a page and hope you can explain it all to your audience.

The solution isn't to eliminate details, but to present them in bites that are small enough to absorb. Sure, this will increase the number of pages in your presentation but, whenever this worries you, just remember this mantra:

"It takes the same amount of time to present five ideas on one slide as it does to present one idea on five slides."

This example demonstrates what I mean. The visual on top shows how the information was captured on paper. I'll grant you that if you were just distributing this on paper; the page might work, since, in this circumstance, the reader controls the communication. He or she can take as much time as needed to review all the information.

However, for an onscreen presentation to an audience, where you, the speaker, control the communication, I would suggest using six legible slides, with each slide comparing the competitor's approach to one of the components of the business system.

An added benefit of this approach is that the audience focuses on one idea at a time, as it is presented. There is no risk that some will focus on different aspects of the visual than the point you're discussing.

Yet another benefit: because there's less information on each visual, we can use a larger type to fill the screen and ensure legibility.

THE BUSINESS SYSTEM FOR EARTH-MOVING EQUIPMENT

Business system element	Technology	Product design	Manufacturing	Sales/ marketing	Distribution	Service
Company A	• Own technology	• Limited engineering investment because CAT works with the best suppliers to create their equipment	• Subcontracted, with CAT doing assembly	• Heavy investment • Sell to broad market • Competitive pricing	• Extensive dealer network	• Fast repair time
Company B	• Own technology	• High engineering investment to design to their own equipment	• Vertically integrated for a large percent of their equipment parts	• Limited investment • Sell to asset-intensive segments • Competitive pricing	• Limited dealer network	• Low frequency of equipment breakdown

---

COMPETING IN EARTH-MOVING EQUIPMENT

Technology | Product design | Manufacturing | Sales/ marketing | Distribution | Service

Company A	Company B
Own technology	Own technology

Different is better

In this solution, we scrap the chart form we had been using entirely and use a completely different form—one more appropriate for the data we're trying to convey.

For instance, while the top chart on the facing page is certainly simple, I find it difficult to determine its message. Can you figure out which country's margins are rising or falling without reading the data at the top of the columns? Also, is there any logic to the sequence of countries?

With such charts, it's helpful to go back to the matrix at the beginning of this book to determine which chart form might be more effective. In this case, we're comparing profit margins for six countries over time. A column chart is often appropriate for a "time comparison," but if you switch to a line chart, use a larger scale, and put the countries in descending order, the trends become clearer. Now the audience can quickly see which countries have the highest margins and where the trends are going.

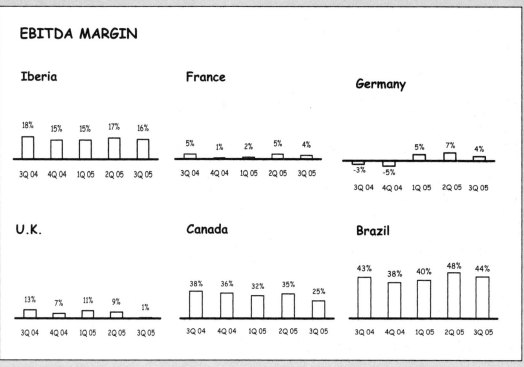

EBITDA MARGIN

Iberia
18% | 15% | 15% | 17% | 16%
3Q 04 | 4Q 04 | 1Q 05 | 2Q 05 | 3Q 05

France
5% | 1% | 2% | 5% | 4%
3Q 04 | 4Q 04 | 1Q 05 | 2Q 05 | 3Q 05

Germany
-3% | -5% | 5% | 7% | 4%
3Q 04 | 4Q 04 | 1Q 05 | 2Q 05 | 3Q 05

U.K.
13% | 7% | 11% | 9% | 1%
3Q 04 | 4Q 04 | 1Q 05 | 2Q 05 | 3Q 05

Canada
38% | 36% | 32% | 35% | 25%
3Q 04 | 4Q 04 | 1Q 05 | 2Q 05 | 3Q 05

Brazil
43% | 38% | 40% | 48% | 44%
3Q 04 | 4Q 04 | 1Q 05 | 2Q 05 | 3Q 05

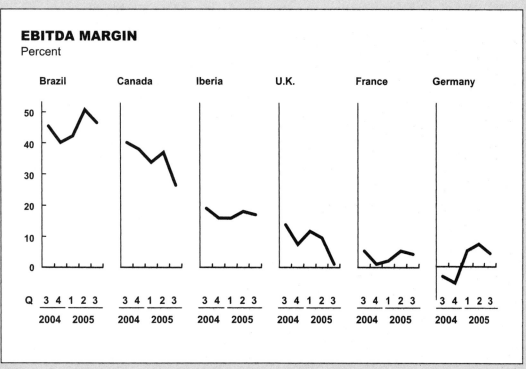

EBITDA MARGIN
Percent

Brazil | Canada | Iberia | U.K. | France | Germany

Q 3 4 1 2 3 | 3 4 1 2 3 | 3 4 1 2 3 | 3 4 1 2 3 | 3 4 1 2 3 | 3 4 1 2 3
2004 2005 | 2004 2005 | 2004 2005 | 2004 2005 | 2004 2005 | 2004 2005

Creativity is better

I would be the first to say that, at times, a basic text slide is all that's needed to convey a message. On the other hand, creative images can help tell your story in a more interesting way, thereby reinforcing understanding. That's what this solution is all about.

For instance, here is a list of recommended steps for planning any business presentation. Since, in this case, there is no set sequence to the order of these steps, and all the steps are independent, I'd suggest that the puzzle image will help make them more memorable.

Furthermore, you can use the puzzle image as a table of contents or "tracker page" to help guide your audience through the chapters of your story. As you move from step to step, you can add each piece of the puzzle. Then, by displaying the entire puzzle at the end, you effectively summarize your main points.

SAY IT WITH PRESENTATIONS

Specify objective

Analyze audience

Define message

Determine scope

Select medium

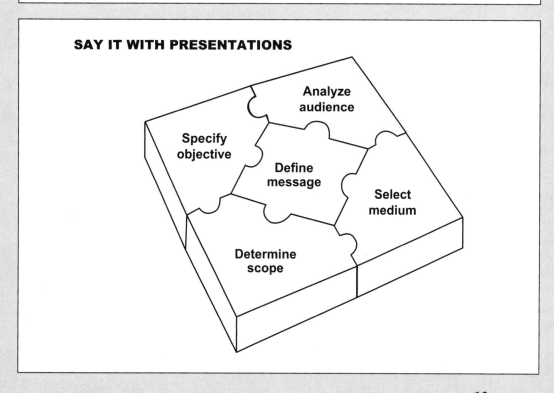

SAY IT WITH PRESENTATIONS

Now it's
YOUR TURN to
Say It with

TRADITIONAL MATERIALS END-USE MARKETS
Percent

Material	Market												
	Aircraft/ aerospace	Recreation/ consumer	Automotive/ transportation	Industrial mechanical	Electrical/ electronic	Petro chemical	Construction/ building	Plumbing	Packaging	Adhesive	Furniture/ furnishings	Other	Total
PVC	--	4	3	--	8	--	64	--	10	2	6	3	100%
PP	--	15	7	--	8	--	--	--	22	--	24	24	100%
HDPE	--	10	5	4	4	--	10	--	52	--	3	12	100%

Your solution

Different is better

Here, we'll assume that the content and its message are well thought through, but that somehow the layout you see— *or don't see*—is simply illegible.

Now let's be clear: if the chart is important enough to be presented, then it's important enough to be legible. So what can you think of that would make the chart legible?

Yes, you could remove those columns that show no data, only dashes. However, grant me that that's not going to help very much. Another solution I sometimes hear is to make a chart out of it. But grant me that charts use more space than tabular data do, so that's not the solution here. Yes, you could break the table and make it into two horizontal rows, or for that matter, put it on several pages.

However, in this case the solution is so simple that it often escapes us: simply switch the axes. That's exactly what I did to use the largest possible type to fill the visual, and you can see how the solution is many times more legible.

TRADITIONAL MATERIALS END-USE MARKETS
Percent

Material	Aircraft/ aerospace	Recreation/ consumer	Automotive/ transportation	Industrial mechanical	Electrical/ electronic	Petro chemical	Construction/ building	Plumbing	Packaging	Adhesive	Furniture/ furnishings	Other	Total
PVC	--	4	3	--	8	--	64	--	10	2	6	3	100%
PP	--	15	7	--	8	--	--	--	22	--	24	24	100%
HDPE	--	10	5	4	4	--	10	--	52	--	3	12	100%

TRADITIONAL MATERIALS END-USE MARKETS

Market	Material		
	PVC	PP	HDPE
Aircraft/aerospace	–	–	–
Recreation/consumer	4%	15%	10%
Automotive/transportation	3	7	5
Industrial/mechanical	–	–	4
Electrical/electronic	8	8	4
Petrochemical	–	–	–
Construction/building	64	–	10
Plumbing	–	–	–
Packaging	10	22	52
Adhesive	2	–	–
Furniture/furnishings	6	24	3
Other	3	24	12
Total	**100%**	**100%**	**100%**

Gene's solution

WHOLESALE BANKING BUSINESS

Sales and trading

- Exchange-based cash instruments (e.g., NYSE)
- OTC cash instruments (e.g., FX, most bonds, London stocks)
- Exchange and OTC derivatives
- Customer and proprietary business

Fee-based services — cash, custody, and trust services

- Cash management
- Corporate trust
- CP issuance
- Custody

Risk management

- Credit
- Market
- Funding/liquidity
- Operations
- Environmental

Institutional asset management

- Domestic bond and equity fundamental funds
- Domestic index/structured funds
- Global fundamental funds
- Global index/structured funds
- Cash/FX, real estate, venture, LBO funds

Corporate lending and advisory

- Corporate finance/advisory
- M&A
- Merchant banking
- Underwriting
- Middle market lending and services
- Commercial lending

Your solution

More is better

This chart is actually not bad if you plan to use it in a memo or a report. However, for an onscreen presentation to a large audience, I'd recommend using six slides: the first to introduce the five quadrants, the subsequent five to highlight each quadrant—one at a time. *(See the back of the facing page for subsequent slides.)*

Yes, I feel your resistance. After all, using six slides where we had one seems to suggest more presentation time. But I think you'd agree that the amount of information being presented is exactly the same. So the time it takes to present that information should also be the same.

Using six slides also avoids the problem of audience distraction. They'll focus on the specific point you're making instead of reading other portions of the slide. And using six slides makes this a truly visual visual presentation, where you keep the audience's interest by changing, changing, changing slides versus forcing them to look at the same slide for a boringly long time.

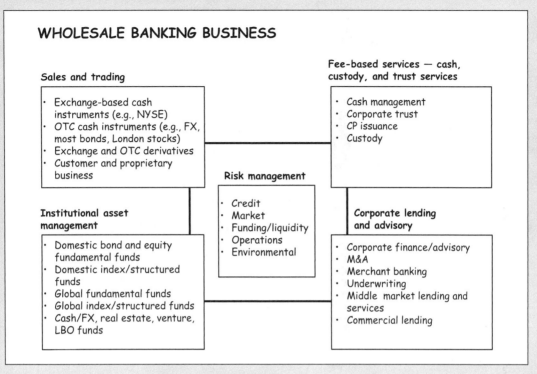

WHOLESALE BANKING BUSINESS

Sales and trading

- Exchange-based cash instruments (e.g., NYSE)
- OTC cash instruments (e.g., FX, most bonds, London stocks)
- Exchange and OTC derivatives
- Customer and proprietary business

Fee-based services — cash, custody, and trust services

- Cash management
- Corporate trust
- CP issuance
- Custody

Risk management

- Credit
- Market
- Funding/liquidity
- Operations
- Environmental

Institutional asset management

- Domestic bond and equity fundamental funds
- Domestic index/structured funds
- Global fundamental funds
- Global index/structured funds
- Cash/FX, real estate, venture, LBO funds

Corporate lending and advisory

- Corporate finance/advisory
- M&A
- Merchant banking
- Underwriting
- Middle market lending and services
- Commercial lending

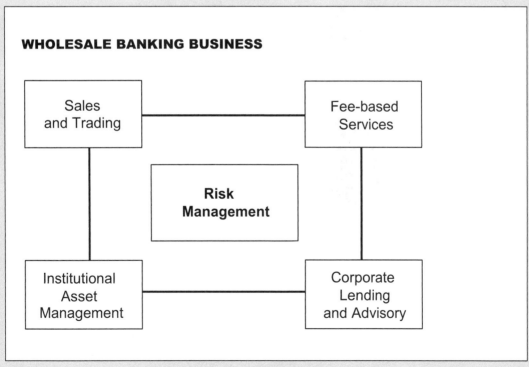

WHOLESALE BANKING BUSINESS

- Sales and Trading
- Fee-based Services
- Risk Management
- Institutional Asset Management
- Corporate Lending and Advisory

Gene's solution

23

WHOLESALE BANKING BUSINESS

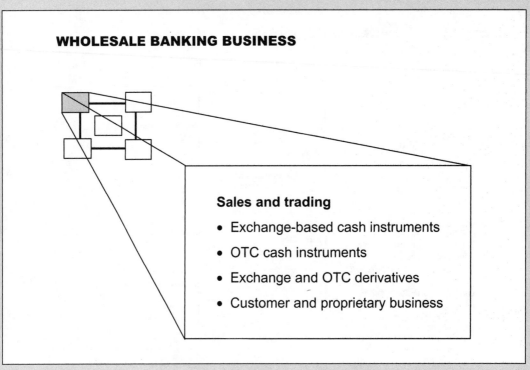

Sales and trading

- Exchange-based cash instruments
- OTC cash instruments
- Exchange and OTC derivatives
- Customer and proprietary business

WHOLESALE BANKING BUSINESS

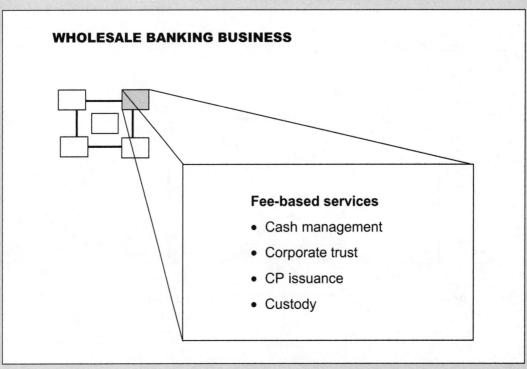

Fee-based services

- Cash management
- Corporate trust
- CP issuance
- Custody

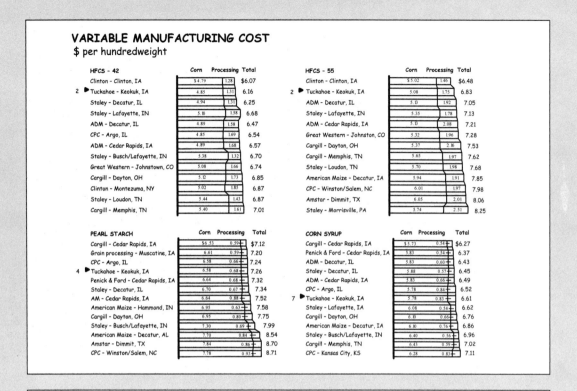

VARIABLE MANUFACTURING COST
$ per hundredweight

HFCS - 42	Corn	Processing	Total
Clinton - Clinton, IA	$4.79	1.28	$6.07
2 ▶ Tuckahoe - Keokuk, IA	4.85	1.31	6.16
Staley - Decatur, IL	4.94	1.31	6.25
Staley - Lafayette, IN	5.10	1.58	6.68
ADM - Decatur, IL	4.89	1.58	6.47
CPC - Argo, IL	4.85	1.69	6.54
ADM - Cedar Rapids, IA	4.89	1.68	6.57
Staley - Busch/Lafayette, IN	5.38	1.32	6.70
Great Western - Johnstown, CO	5.08	1.66	6.74
Cargill - Dayton, OH	5.12	1.73	6.85
Clinton - Montezuma, NY	5.02	1.85	6.87
Staley - Loudon, TN	5.44	1.43	6.87
Cargill - Memphis, TN	5.40	1.61	7.01

HFCS - 55	Corn	Processing	Total
Clinton - Clinton, IA	$5.02	1.46	$6.48
2 ▶ Tuckahoe - Keokuk, IA	5.08	1.75	6.83
ADM - Decatur, IL	5.13	1.92	7.05
Staley - Lafayette, IN	5.35	1.78	7.13
ADM - Cedar Rapids, IA	5.13	2.08	7.21
Great Western - Johnston, CO	5.32	1.96	7.28
Cargill - Dayton, OH	5.37	2.16	7.53
Cargill - Memphis, TN	5.65	1.97	7.62
Staley - Loudon, TN	5.70	1.98	7.68
American Maize - Decatur, IA	5.94	1.91	7.85
CPC - Winston/Salem, NC	6.01	1.97	7.98
Amstar - Dimmit, TX	6.05	2.01	8.06
Staley - Morrisville, PA	5.74	2.51	8.25

PEARL STARCH	Corn	Processing	Total
Cargill - Cedar Rapids, IA	$6.53	0.59	$7.12
Grain processing - Muscatine, IA	6.61	0.59	7.20
CPC - Argo, IL	6.58	0.66	7.24
4 ▶ Tuckahoe - Keokuk, IA	6.58	0.68	7.26
Penick & Ford - Cedar Rapids, IA	6.64	0.68	7.32
Staley - Decatur, IL	6.70	0.67	7.34
AM - Cedar Rapids, IA	6.64	0.88	7.52
American Maize - Hammond, IN	6.95	0.63	7.58
Cargill - Dayton, OH	6.95	0.80	7.75
Staley - Busch/Lafayette, IN	7.30	0.69	7.99
American Maize - Decatur, AL	7.70	0.84	8.54
Amstar - Dimmit, TX	7.84	0.86	8.70
CPC - Winston/Salem, NC	7.78	0.93	8.71

CORN SYRUP	Corn	Processing	Total
Cargill - Cedar Rapids, IA	$5.73	0.54	$6.27
Penick & Ford - Cedar Rapids, IA	5.83	0.54	6.37
ADM - Decatur, IL	5.83	0.60	6.43
Staley - Decatur, IL	5.88	0.57	6.45
ADM - Cedar Rapids, IA	5.83	0.66	6.49
CPC - Argo, IL	5.78	0.84	6.52
7 ▶ Tuckahoe - Keokuk, IA	5.78	0.83	6.61
Staley - Lafayette, IA	6.08	0.54	6.62
Cargill - Dayton, OH	6.10	0.66	6.76
American Maize - Decatur, IA	6.10	0.76	6.86
Staley - Busch/Lafayette, IN	6.40	0.56	6.96
Cargill - Memphis, TN	6.43	0.59	7.02
CPC - Kansas City, KS	6.28	0.83	7.11

Your solution

Simpler and different are better

At times, the obvious solution of splitting one detailed chart into several isn't the answer to legibility. Sometimes, just reducing the amount of detail and highlighting the most important component of the story can result in a major improvement.

Follow the story: *"This chart shows that the Tuckahoe plant is doing an excellent job of keeping variable costs low in the manufacture of three out of four products. For HFCS-42 and HFCS-55, it ranks as the second-lowest-cost producer. While it ranks fourth for pearl starch, the cost differential with the lowest-cost plant is small. However, for corn syrup, the combination of a seventh ranking and a sizable cost differential indicates the need to search for cost-reduction opportunities."*

For the visual presentation, the most obvious solution would be to use a separate slide for each product. However, with as many as 13 horizontal bars for each, the plant names would probably still be illegible. And creating four separate pages would prevent the audience from easily comparing the four products.

In this case, the answer is to "visualize the message, not the mess." The important elements of the message here are: performance and Tuckahoe ranking. We use a range column chart to show the spread in total variable cost between the best and worst performers for the four products. Here, the ranges are the same length, creating an index chart; that is, the spread equals 100 regardless of the cost differentials. We show Tuckahoe's ranking against the top and bottom performers. The message comes across with one clear and legible chart. If you feel the need to provide the detailed data, just distribute the original chart as part of any handouts you leave behind with your audience.

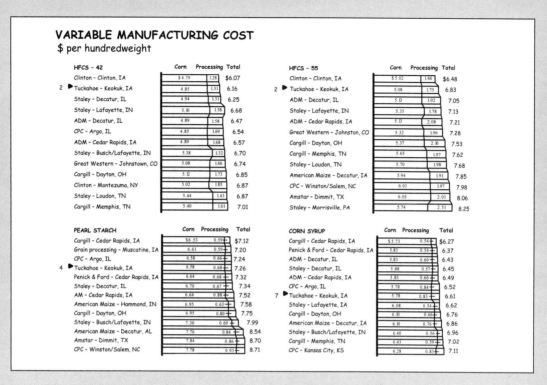

VARIABLE MANUFACTURING COST
$ per hundredweight

HFCS – 42

	Corn	Processing	Total
Clinton – Clinton, IA	$4.79	1.28	$6.07
2 Tuckahoe – Keokuk, IA	4.85	1.31	6.16
Staley – Decatur, IL	4.94	1.31	6.25
Staley – Lafayette, IN	5.10	1.58	6.68
ADM – Decatur, IL	4.89	1.58	6.47
CPC – Argo, IL	4.85	1.69	6.54
ADM – Cedar Rapids, IA	4.89	1.68	6.57
Staley – Busch/Lafayette, IN	5.38	1.32	6.70
Great Western – Johnstown, CO	5.08	1.66	6.74
Cargill – Dayton, OH	5.12	1.73	6.85
Clinton – Montezuma, NY	5.02	1.85	6.87
Staley – Loudon, TN	5.44	1.43	6.87
Cargill – Memphis, TN	5.40	1.61	7.01

HFCS – 55

	Corn	Processing	Total
Clinton – Clinton, IA	$5.02	1.46	$6.48
2 Tuckahoe – Keokuk, IA	5.08	1.75	6.83
ADM – Decatur, IL	5.13	1.92	7.05
Staley – Lafayette, IN	5.35	1.78	7.13
ADM – Cedar Rapids, IA	5.13	2.08	7.21
Great Western – Johnston, CO	5.32	1.96	7.28
Cargill – Dayton, OH	5.37	2.16	7.53
Cargill – Memphis, TN	5.65	1.97	7.62
Staley – Loudon, TN	5.70	1.98	7.68
American Maize – Decatur, IA	5.94	1.91	7.85
CPC – Winston/Salem, NC	6.01	1.97	7.98
Amstar – Dimmit, TX	6.05	2.01	8.06
Staley – Morrisville, PA	5.74	2.51	8.25

PEARL STARCH

	Corn	Processing	Total
Cargill – Cedar Rapids, IA	$6.53	0.59	$7.12
Grain processing – Muscatine, IA	6.61	0.59	7.20
CPC – Argo, IL	6.58	0.66	7.24
4 Tuckahoe – Keokuk, IA	6.58	0.68	7.26
Penick & Ford – Cedar Rapids, IA	6.64	0.68	7.32
Staley – Decatur, IL	6.70	0.67	7.34
AM – Cedar Rapids, IA	6.64	0.88	7.52
American Maize – Hammond, IN	6.95	0.63	7.58
Cargill – Dayton, OH	6.95	0.80	7.75
Staley – Busch/Lafayette, IN	7.30	0.69	7.99
American Maize – Decatur, AL	7.70	0.84	8.54
Amstar – Dimmit, TX	7.84	0.86	8.70
CPC – Winston/Salem, NC	7.78	0.93	8.71

CORN SYRUP

	Corn	Processing	Total
Cargill – Cedar Rapids, IA	$5.73	0.54	$6.27
Penick & Ford – Cedar Rapids, IA	5.83	0.54	6.37
ADM – Decatur, IL	5.83	0.60	6.43
Staley – Decatur, IL	5.88	0.57	6.45
ADM – Cedar Rapids, IA	5.83	0.66	6.49
CPC – Argo, IL	5.78	0.84	6.52
7 Tuckahoe – Keokuk, IA	5.78	0.83	6.61
Staley – Lafayette, IA	6.08	0.54	6.62
Cargill – Dayton, OH	6.10	0.66	6.76
American Maize – Decatur, IA	6.10	0.76	6.86
Staley – Busch/Lafayette, IN	6.40	0.56	6.96
Cargill – Memphis, TN	6.43	0.59	7.02
CPC – Kansas City, KS	6.28	0.83	7.11

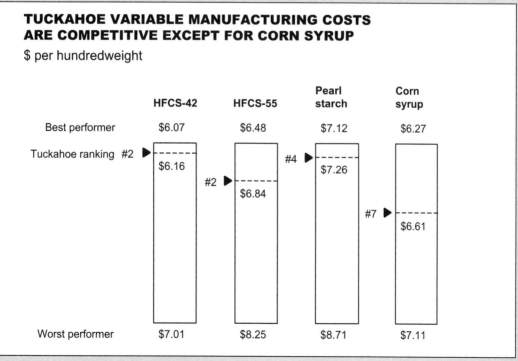

TUCKAHOE VARIABLE MANUFACTURING COSTS ARE COMPETITIVE EXCEPT FOR CORN SYRUP

$ per hundredweight

	HFCS-42	HFCS-55	Pearl starch	Corn syrup
Best performer	$6.07	$6.48	$7.12	$6.27
Tuckahoe ranking	#2 $6.16	#2 $6.84	#4 $7.26	#7 $6.61
Worst performer	$7.01	$8.25	$8.71	$7.11

Gene's solution

27

QTURN **TRANSFORMATION THEMES**

- Capture regional and domestic growth

- Achieve first-class operational efficiency and effectiveness

- Strengthen financial structure

- Earn customer loyalty

- Attract and develop the most talented people

- Enable Qcompany's development

Your solution

Creativity is better

This one took me a while to figure out, but the impact was worth the effort.

The solution came to me once I saw that the company's name, at the bottom of the list, started with the letter "Q," and that the logo-like symbol in the title began with a "Q."

It became clear that the "Q" needed to dominate the visual. I was able to place the bullet points so the most important theme was at the center of the diagram and to position another theme at the bottom of the "Q," reinforcing the image of movement over time.

I'm often asked how these ideas come to mind. Like anything else, the more you exercise your creativity, the more skillful you become. Practice, practice, practice!

Q<small>TURN</small> TRANSFORMATION THEMES

- Capture regional and domestic growth

- Achieve first-class operational efficiency and effectiveness

- Strengthen financial structure

- Earn customer loyalty

- Attract and develop the most talented people

- Enable Qcompany's development

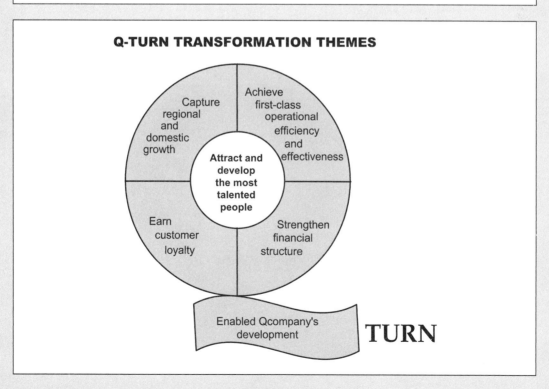

Q-TURN TRANSFORMATION THEMES

Gene's solution

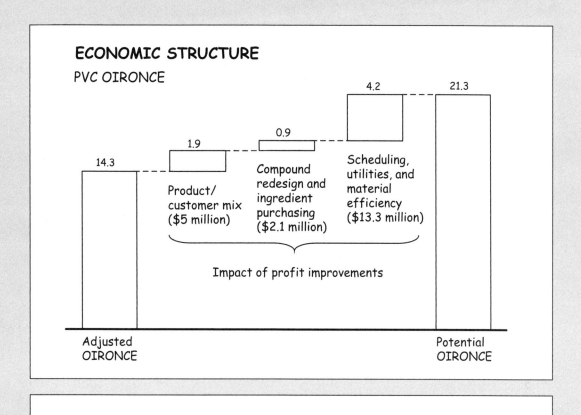

ECONOMIC STRUCTURE

PVC OIRONCE

4.2

21.3

1.9

0.9

14.3

Product/
customer mix
($5 million)

Compound
redesign and
ingredient
purchasing
($2.1 million)

Scheduling,
utilities, and
material
efficiency
($13.3 million)

Impact of profit improvements

Adjusted
OIRONCE

Potential
OIRONCE

Different is better

I'm with you if you feel this chart might suffice in many cases. It's a typical example of a "waterfall" chart, showing the parts of a whole.

However, it strikes me as unnecessarily busy: I'm not getting a clear indication of the sum of the improvements; I'd like the dollars of improvements to line up; I don't need to repeat the **OIRONCE** label at the bottom of both columns, since it's introduced in the subtitle. All of this argues for using a different chart form.

By combining the profit improvement into one subdivided column chart, the labels line up and the dollars stack up to their total.

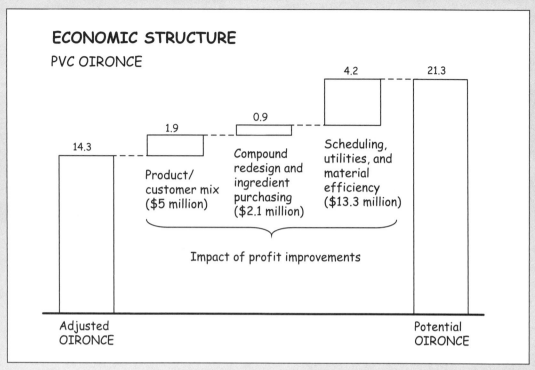

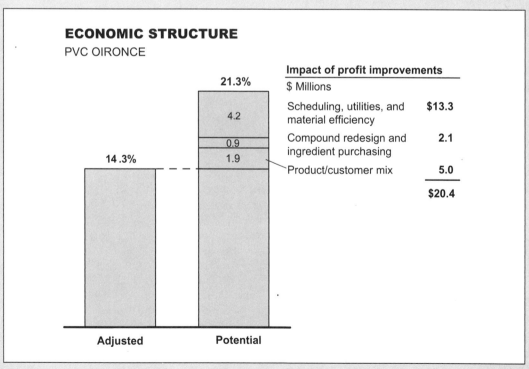

Gene's solution

COST STRUCTURE BY MARKET SEGMENT

Segment A Client

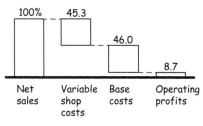

Competitor

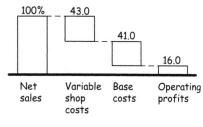

Segment B Client

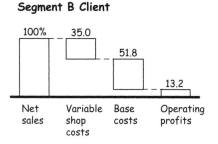

Competitor

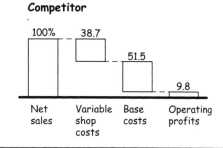

Your solution

Different is better

Once more, the waterfall chart is at work here, but this one strikes me as even busier than the last.

The scale is so squeezed that the differences in the plotted values are difficult to measure. In addition, the labels at the bottom of the columns are redundant. Most importantly, the chart doesn't accomplish its main goal: allowing the audience to easily compare the company and its competitor in each of the two segments.

By placing the components within 100 percent columns, I can use a much bigger scale, I limit the number of labels, and I line up the data in a way that allows an easy comparison.

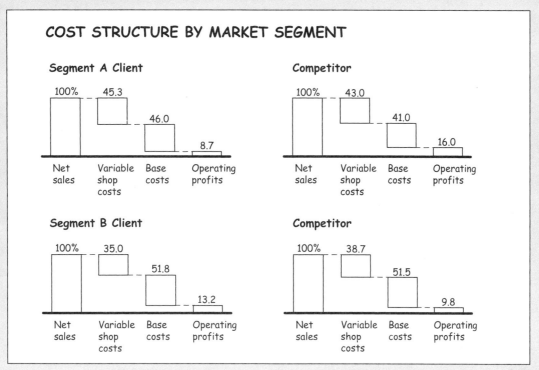

COST STRUCTURE BY MARKET SEGMENT

Segment A Client

100% — 45.3 — 46.0 — 8.7

Net sales | Variable shop costs | Base costs | Operating profits

Competitor

100% — 43.0 — 41.0 — 16.0

Net sales | Variable shop costs | Base costs | Operating profits

Segment B Client

100% — 35.0 — 51.8 — 13.2

Net sales | Variable shop costs | Base costs | Operating profits

Competitor

100% — 38.7 — 51.5 — 9.8

Net sales | Variable shop costs | Base costs | Operating profits

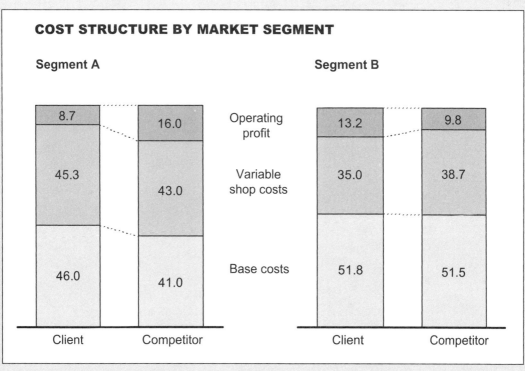

COST STRUCTURE BY MARKET SEGMENT

Segment A

| | Operating profit | | | Variable shop costs | | | Base costs | |

Client: 8.7 / 45.3 / 46.0
Competitor: 16.0 / 43.0 / 41.0

Segment B

Client: 13.2 / 35.0 / 51.8
Competitor: 9.8 / 38.7 / 51.5

Client | Competitor

Gene's solution

39

COMPANY A VS. COMPETITION ATTRIBUTE RATINGS
Percent

Good food attributes	Co. A	Co. B	Co. C	Co. D	Co. E
Food tastes good	60%	76%	68%	78%	54%
They use only the highest quality ingredients	50	63	53	71	43
They serve food that people serve at home	54	61	43	48	49
Most of the food is cooked to order	61	65	60	69	64

Different is better

I'll grant that there are those in the business community who "inhale" tabular data. That is, they look at a list of numbers and quickly read the trends they represent. However, as I point out in *Say It with Charts*, data implies relationships, whereas charts demonstrate them. And so it is with this example.

In this case, by plotting the range between the low and high performers for each of the attributes, we see Company A's ranking much more quickly and without needing to read and interpret all the numbers in the table.

COMPANY A VS. COMPETITION ATTRIBUTE RATINGS
Percent

Good food attributes	Co. A	Co. B	Co. C	Co. D	Co. E
Food tastes good	60%	76%	68%	78%	54%
They use only the highest quality ingredients	50	63	53	71	43
They serve food that people serve at home	54	61	43	48	49
Most of the food is cooked to order	61	65	60	69	64

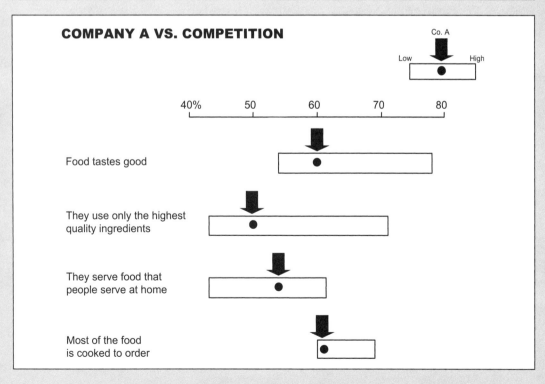

COMPANY A VS. COMPETITION

Gene's solution

DIFFERENCES IN EMERGING MARKETS

Developed markets

- Problem accounts under control
- Banks operate based on risk-adjusted profits
- Practices and policies to ensure accurate information
- Known sources of risk

vs.

Emerging markets

- Large number of problem accounts
- Performance assessment based on volume or net profits
- Information is not available/accurate
- Unknown/unqualifiable services of risk (i.e., complex cross-share holdings)

Proposed solution

- Process to systematically address large number of loans
- Tools to assist in data collection and decision making
- Organization compartments to support process

Your solution

45

Creativity is better

On the surface, it's hard to see why we would want to change the chart at the top of the next page. After all, it does a good job of showing how the proposed solution comes out of the differences identified between the developed and emerging markets.

And yet, for me, the word "Differences" in the title made me feel that the solution resulted from the combined forces at work—therefore what you see on the bottom chart.

The added benefits are that the visual looks more attractive as a design, and it makes it stand out from the crowd of other visuals we traditionally see in presentations.

DIFFERENCES IN EMERGING MARKETS

Developed markets

- Problem accounts under control
- Banks operate based on risk-adjusted profits
- Practices and policies to ensure accurate information
- Known sources of risk

vs.

Emerging markets

- Large number of problem accounts
- Performance assessment based on volume or net profits
- Information is not available/accurate
- Unknown/unqualifiable services of risk (i.e., complex cross-share holdings)

Proposed solution

- Process to systematically address large number of loans
- Tools to assist in data collection and decision making
- Organization compartments to support process

DIFFERENCES IN EMERGING MARKETS

PROPOSED SOLUTION

- Process to systematically address large number of loans
- Tools to assist in data collection and decision making
- Organization compartments to support process

DEVELOPED MARKETS

- Problem accounts under control
- Banks operate based on risk-adjusted profits
- Practices and policies to ensure accurate information
- Known sources of risk

 vs.

EMERGING MARKETS

- Large number of problem accounts
- Performance based on volume or net profits
- Information is not available/accurate
- Unknown/unqualifiable services of risk

Gene's solution

47

COMPARING APPROACHES

> **Same objective**
> Expand beyond LD to capture
> more revenue/profit

Different
approaches

COMPANY A
"Get as much footprint as quickly as possible given
financial constraints, through opportunistic and
uncertain alliances"

COMPANY B
"Expand from core competencies while
retaining control along the way"

• Make opportunistic moves through small investments/acquisitions and alliances	vs.	• Make big bests through large investments and acquisitions
• Resell and form alliances with established players	vs.	• Build own capabilities
• Extend reach through alliances, JVs	vs.	• Use own distribution
• Have strong partners well established in their areas of expertise	vs.	• Have weaker partners who can be better influenced
• Reach large customer segments, with an increasing consumer orientation	vs.	• Target fewer high-value customers to sell more things to

Fast and opportunistic
moves, with potential
execution challenges

> **Growing, changing, and
> uncertain markets?**

Planned approach aiming for
wholly owned perfect answers
and customer control

Your solution

Resist the temptation
to sneak a peak

Remember, your solution
may be BETTER than mine

Creativity is better

It doesn't take long to understand that the point of the chart at the top of the next page is to contrast the approaches that the two companies take to reach the same objective.

However, I find myself spending too much valuable time reading all the bullet points to be able to appreciate the distinctions the chart describes and the flow of ideas.

My solution, shown below the first chart, is to switch the flow from top–bottom to bottom–top. In this manner, the chart first identifies the forces at work (growing, changing, uncertain markets) that lead to a summary of each company's approach, seen at the base of the arrows. Then, the eye moves up to see a simpler and clearer contrast of each company's moves, all of which leads to the common objective at the top.

Adding the arrows in perspective helps the eyes follow the flow.

A general tip is worthy of mention here: arrows are powerful tools to convey a number of concepts—changes in a situation, movement, or the passage of time, just to name a few. I use them often to "point the way."

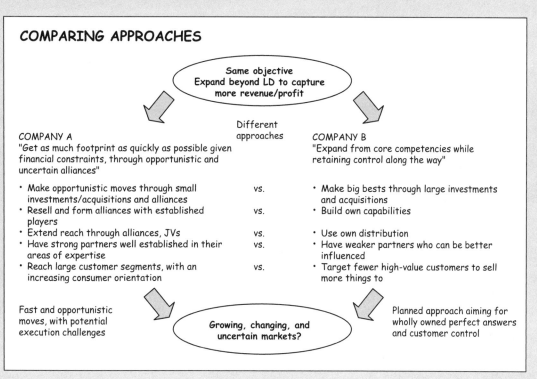

COMPARING APPROACHES

Same objective
Expand beyond LD to capture
more revenue/profit

Different
approaches

COMPANY A
"Get as much footprint as quickly as possible given financial constraints, through opportunistic and uncertain alliances"

COMPANY B
"Expand from core competencies while retaining control along the way"

• Make opportunistic moves through small investments/acquisitions and alliances	vs.	• Make big bests through large investments and acquisitions
• Resell and form alliances with established players	vs.	• Build own capabilities
• Extend reach through alliances, JVs	vs.	• Use own distribution
• Have strong partners well established in their areas of expertise	vs.	• Have weaker partners who can be better influenced
• Reach large customer segments, with an increasing consumer orientation	vs.	• Target fewer high-value customers to sell more things to

Fast and opportunistic moves, with potential execution challenges

Growing, changing, and uncertain markets?

Planned approach aiming for wholly owned perfect answers and customer control

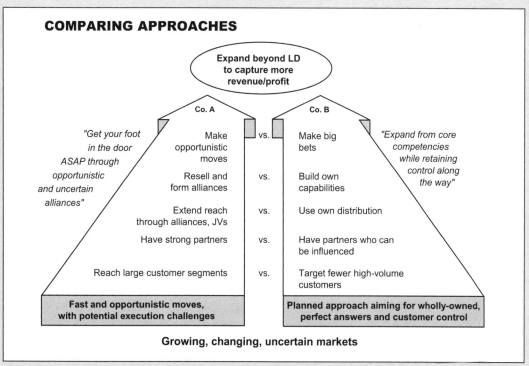

COMPARING APPROACHES

Expand beyond LD
to capture more
revenue/profit

Co. A

Co. B

"Get your foot in the door ASAP through opportunistic and uncertain alliances"

Make opportunistic moves	vs.	Make big bets
Resell and form alliances	vs.	Build own capabilities
Extend reach through alliances, JVs	vs.	Use own distribution
Have strong partners	vs.	Have partners who can be influenced
Reach large customer segments	vs.	Target fewer high-volume customers

"Expand from core competencies while retaining control along the way"

Fast and opportunistic moves, with potential execution challenges

Planned approach aiming for wholly-owned, perfect answers and customer control

Growing, changing, uncertain markets

Gene's solution

53

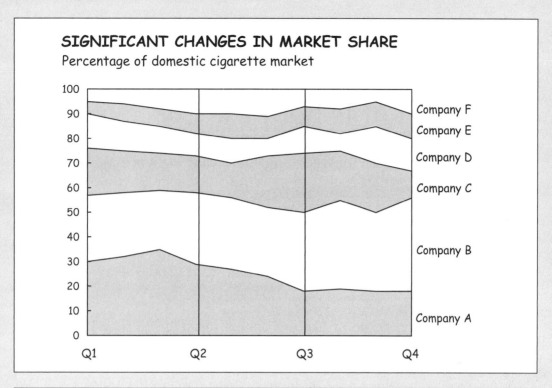

SIGNIFICANT CHANGES IN MARKET SHARE
Percentage of domestic cigarette market

Your solution

Different is better

One of the criteria for designing charts that work is making sure that the chart clearly depicts the message in the title.

In this case, I just don't experience the word "significant."

I do see the decline over the year for Company A because it's measured against a flat base line. But what about the other companies?

Can you appreciate the difference that results from showing each company against its own base line? Also, notice that by squeezing the time scale and making better use of the layout space, we're able to use a bigger scale that magnifies the "significant" differences mentioned in the title.

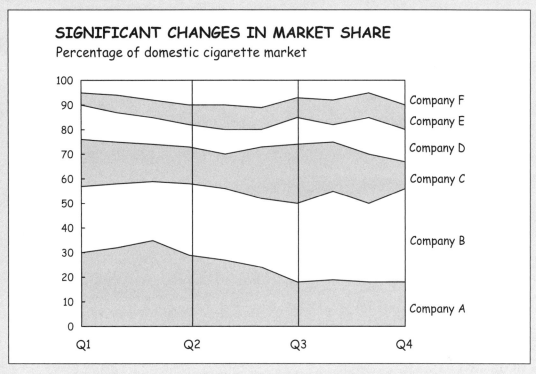

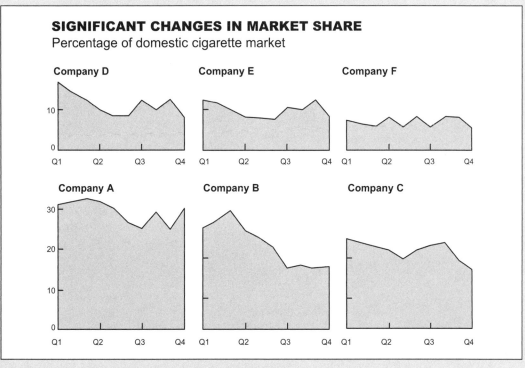

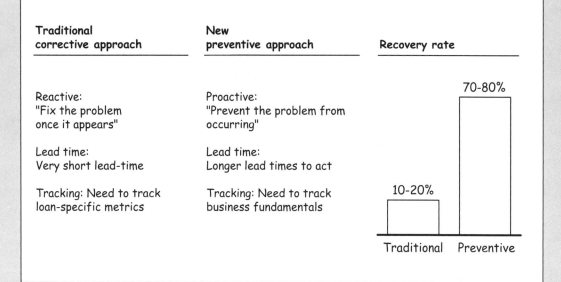

TRADITIONAL "CORRECTIVE" APPROACH VS. NEW "PREVENTIVE" APPROACH

Traditional corrective approach

Reactive:
"Fix the problem once it appears"

Lead time:
Very short lead-time

Tracking: Need to track loan-specific metrics

New preventive approach

Proactive:
"Prevent the problem from occurring"

Lead time:
Longer lead times to act

Tracking: Need to track business fundamentals

Recovery rate

70-80%

10-20%

Traditional   Preventive

Your solution

Creativity is better

Once more, an example of a chart that's easy to follow
and that doesn't appear to need change.

However, did you notice the back-and-forth movement
of your eyes as you sought to figure out the relationship
of the column chart at the right with the column headings
on the left?

Can you now appreciate the added benefit of the arrows,
which more quickly distinguish the opposite direction of
the two approaches and lead to the corresponding "recovery
rate" resulting from each approach?

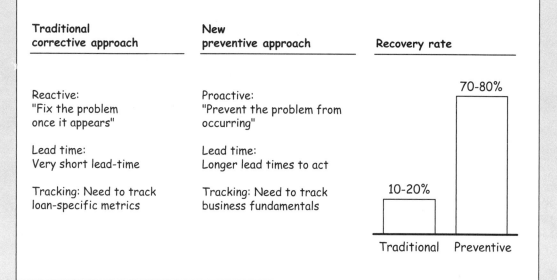

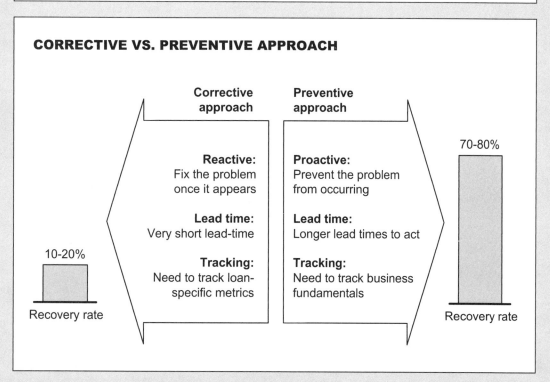

Gene's solution

ETHICAL PHARMACEUTICAL MARKET GROWTH

Sources of change CAGR, percent

Market	Volume	Price	Mix		Total
			Generics	Innovation/other	
U.S.	1.7	7.9	-0.5	3.6	13.2
Germany	1.0	1.0	-0.6	5.0	6.5
U.K.	1.8	0.8	-1.1	9.2	10.8
France	3.4	-1.5	-0.1	10.0	12.0
Italy	0.8	1.1	-0.2	15.6	17.6
Japan	5.0	-0.4	0.0	5.3	6.2
Total	3.2	1.2	-0.3	5.7	10.0

Your solution

Different is better

Here's an example showing that plotting every number results in hardly any visual difference among the data. It renders the chart frustratingly difficult to read, especially because the scale is so squeezed.

In this case, I plotted just the totals in a vertical bar chart and then left the rest of the data in a table underneath its respective country. In this manner, we can see the range of growth by country and then study the sources that contribute to the change in a much more restful table.

By the way, the sequence of columns could have been arranged in either descending or ascending order, depending on the situation at hand. Granted that this is an "item comparison" that should be treated more often than not as a horizontal bar chart. Let's be flexible in this case and agree that the vertical bars work better.

This chart provides a good illustration of a solution that is sometimes so obvious we don't see it. We frequently feel obligated to plot our data in bars, columns, or whatever, when the best idea may be to just "table it."

ETHICAL PHARMACEUTICAL MARKET GROWTH

Sources of change CAGR, percent

Market	Volume	Price	Mix		Total
			Generics	Innovation/other	
U.S.	1.7	7.9	-0.5	3.6	13.2
Germany	1.0	1.0	-0.6	5.0	6.5
U.K.	1.8	0.8	-1.1	9.2	10.8
France	3.4	-1.5	-0.1	10.0	12.0
Italy	0.8	1.1	-0.2	15.6	17.6
Japan	5.0	-0.4	0.0	5.3	6.2
Total	3.2	1.2	-0.3	5.7	10.0

ETHICAL PHARMACEUTICAL MARKET GROWTH

CAGR 2003-2005

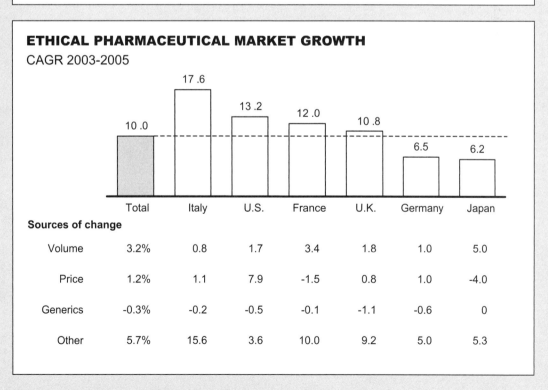

	Total	Italy	U.S.	France	U.K.	Germany	Japan
	10.0	17.6	13.2	12.0	10.8	6.5	6.2

Sources of change

	Total	Italy	U.S.	France	U.K.	Germany	Japan
Volume	3.2%	0.8	1.7	3.4	1.8	1.0	5.0
Price	1.2%	1.1	7.9	-1.5	0.8	1.0	-4.0
Generics	-0.3%	-0.2	-0.5	-0.1	-1.1	-0.6	0
Other	5.7%	15.6	3.6	10.0	9.2	5.0	5.3

Gene's solution

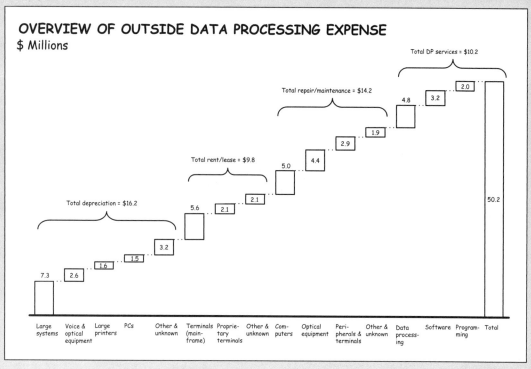

OVERVIEW OF OUTSIDE DATA PROCESSING EXPENSE
$ Millions

Total depreciation = $16.2

Total rent/lease = $9.8

Total repair/maintenance = $14.2

Total DP services = $10.2

7.3	Large systems
2.6	Voice & optical equipment
1.6	Large printers
1.5	PCs
3.2	Other & unknown
5.6	Terminals (mainframe)
2.1	Proprietary terminals
2.1	Other & unknown
5.0	Computers
4.4	Optical equipment
2.9	Peripherals & terminals
1.9	Other & unknown
4.8	Data processing
3.2	Software
2.0	Programming
50.2	Total

Your solution

67

Different is better

Waterfall charts work best when they are used to show a combination of pluses and minuses. Otherwise, they demonstrate the first habit of bad chart design: "Nothing is ever so simple that we cannot make it complex."

Can you see—or not see—that all we have here is a pie chart showing how the parts add up to the total? On the other hand, given the number of components in this case, I'll grant that a pie chart would not work. Therefore, make it into an "item comparison" and create four clusters of bar charts.

Now you can use a much larger scale to differentiate the data. And notice how the labels are **much easier to read**, since they're no longer limited by the width of the columns.

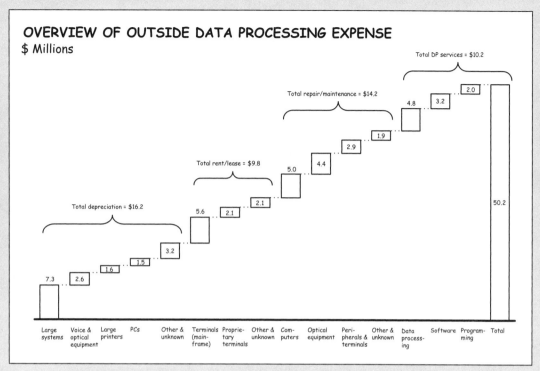

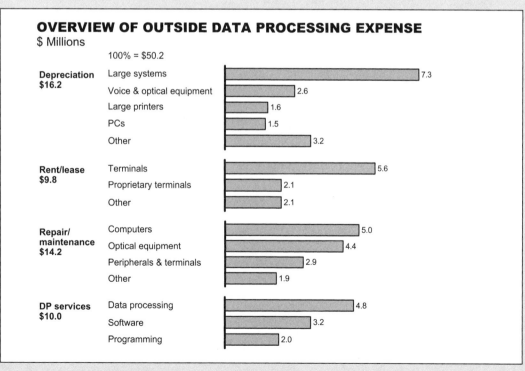

Gene's solution

TYPICAL MANAGEMENT ACTIONS TO DRIVE SALES PERFORMANCE SOMETIMES MISS THE MARK

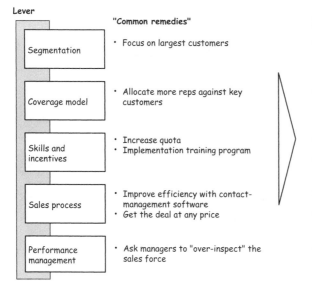

Lever

"Common remedies"

Reality

Segmentation
- Focus on largest customers
- Large customers not always most profitable

Coverage model
- Allocate more reps against key customers
- 20-30% productivity improvement possible from current reps

Skills and incentives
- Increase quota
- Implementation training program
- Can drive short-term growth at cost of customer satisfaction
- Without coaching, majority of benefit lost within one month

Sales process
- Improve efficiency with contact-management software
- Get the deal at any price
- Limited impact without behavioral change
- Actual margin often negative for >50% of customers

Performance management
- Ask managers to "over-inspect" the sales force
- Most managers overburdened with metrics/meetings

Your solution

71

More is better

I'd like to believe that by now you can quickly figure
out what to do with this one.

As before, this chart works well on a single page as a
handout.

But for an onscreen presentation—no matter the pressure
to minimize the number of slides—breaking it into multiple
slides concentrates comments on each of the levers one at a
time, and avoids the problem of the audience reading
ahead.

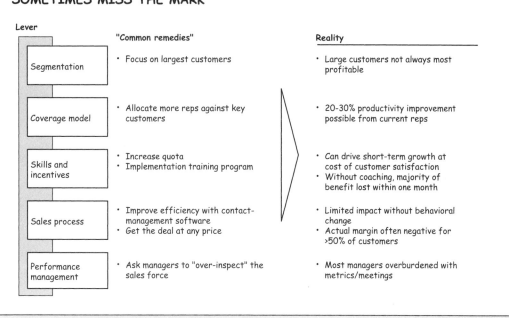

TYPICAL MANAGEMENT ACTIONS TO DRIVE SALES PERFORMANCE SOMETIMES MISS THE MARK

Lever

Lever	"Common remedies"	Reality
Segmentation	• Focus on largest customers	• Large customers not always most profitable
Coverage model	• Allocate more reps against key customers	• 20-30% productivity improvement possible from current reps
Skills and incentives	• Increase quota • Implementation training program	• Can drive short-term growth at cost of customer satisfaction • Without coaching, majority of benefit lost within one month
Sales process	• Improve efficiency with contact-management software • Get the deal at any price	• Limited impact without behavioral change • Actual margin often negative for >50% of customers
Performance management	• Ask managers to "over-inspect" the sales force	• Most managers overburdened with metrics/meetings

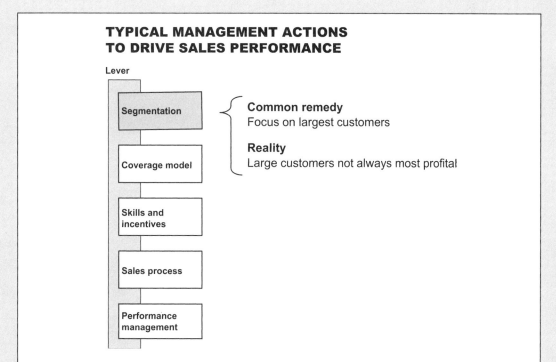

TYPICAL MANAGEMENT ACTIONS TO DRIVE SALES PERFORMANCE

Lever

- Segmentation
- Coverage model
- Skills and incentives
- Sales process
- Performance management

Common remedy
Focus on largest customers

Reality
Large customers not always most profital

Gene's solution

TYPICAL MANAGEMENT ACTIONS
TO DRIVE SALES PERFORMANCE

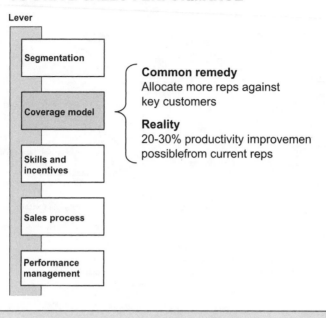

Lever

- Segmentation
- Coverage model
- Skills and incentives
- Sales process
- Performance management

Common remedy
Allocate more reps against key customers

Reality
20-30% productivity improvemen possiblefrom current reps

TYPICAL MANAGEMENT ACTIONS
TO DRIVE SALES PERFORMANCE

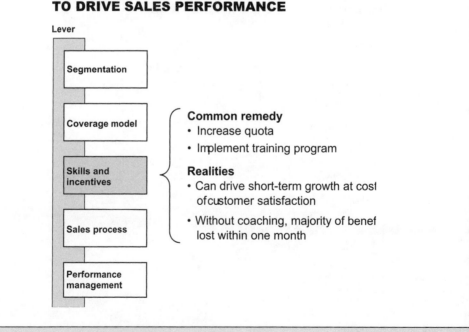

Lever

- Segmentation
- Coverage model
- Skills and incentives
- Sales process
- Performance management

Common remedy
- Increase quota
- Implement training program

Realities
- Can drive short-term growth at cost ofcustomer satisfaction

- Without coaching, majority of benef lost within one month

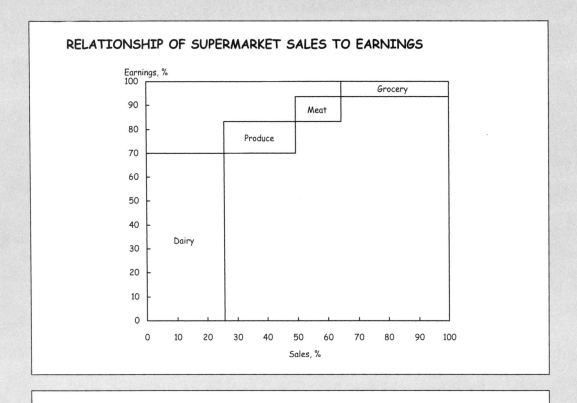

RELATIONSHIP OF SUPERMARKET SALES TO EARNINGS

Earnings, %

Grocery

Meat

Produce

Dairy

Sales, %

Your solution

Different is better

As simple as the chart looks, it takes time to figure out how best to read the information. With a bit of effort, we finally see that this is meant to show the correlation between the percentages of sales to earnings for each of four supermarket product categories.

The same message can be delivered more easily and quickly by using a two-columned chart.

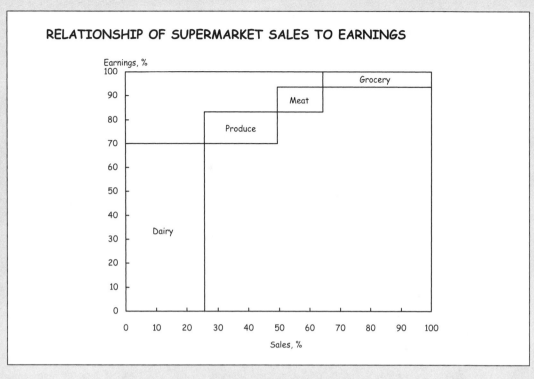

RELATIONSHIP OF SUPERMARKET SALES TO EARNINGS

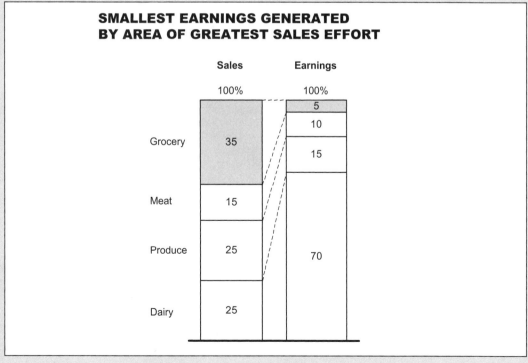

SMALLEST EARNINGS GENERATED
BY AREA OF GREATEST SALES EFFORT

Gene's solution

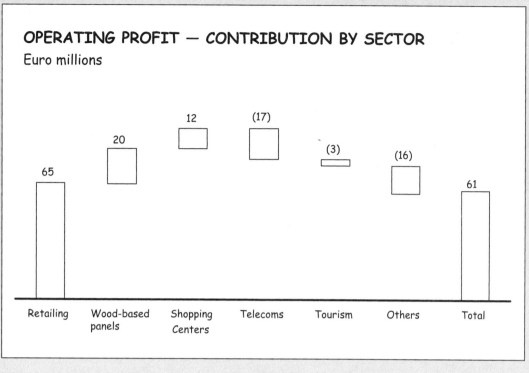

OPERATING PROFIT — CONTRIBUTION BY SECTOR
Euro millions

		12	(17)			
65	20			(3)	(16)	61

| Retailing | Wood-based panels | Shopping Centers | Telecoms | Tourism | Others | Total |

Your solution

Creativity is better

I have two simple suggestions that would make this chart easier to read.

One you see on the bottom, which is to use directional arrows to make it easier to see the ups and downs of the various components.

Second, on the other side of the facing page, is to group all the pluses into one arrow versus the sum of all the minuses, thereby reducing the number of individual components we usually see on these charts.

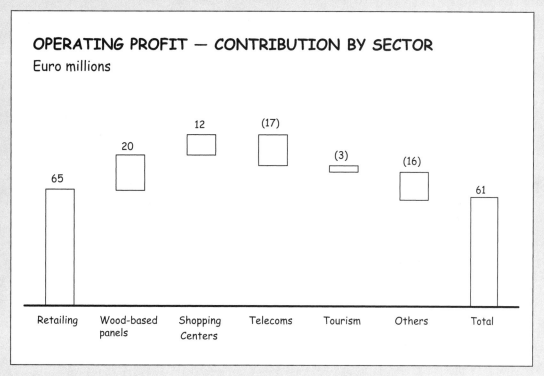

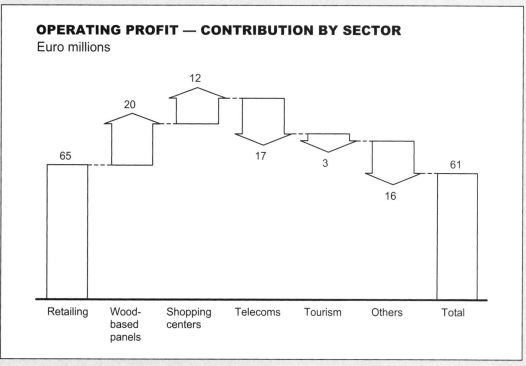

Gene's solution

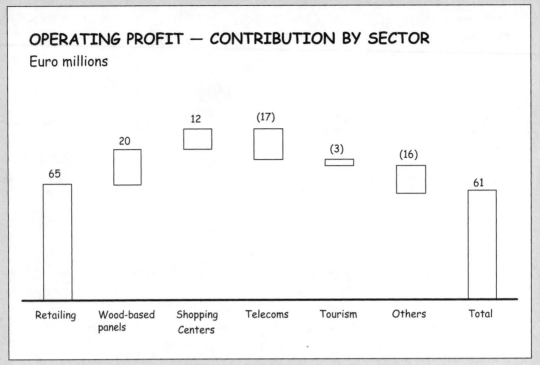

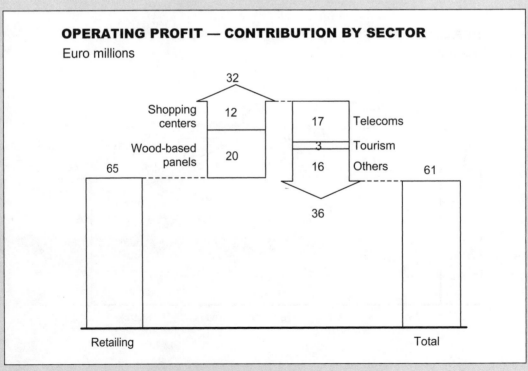

PROBLEMATIC LOANS ARE A GLOBAL CONCERN
U.S. $ Billions

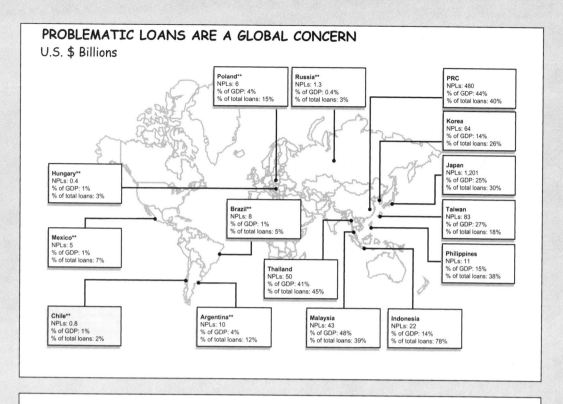

Poland**
NPLs: 6
% of GDP: 4%
% of total loans: 15%

Russia**
NPLs: 1.3
% of GDP: 0.4%
% of total loans: 3%

PRC
NPLs: 480
% of GDP: 44%
% of total loans: 40%

Korea
NPLs: 64
% of GDP: 14%
% of total loans: 26%

Japan
NPLs: 1,201
% of GDP: 25%
% of total loans: 30%

Hungary**
NPLs: 0.4
% of GDP: 1%
% of total loans: 3%

Brazil**
NPLs: 8
% of GDP: 1%
% of total loans: 5%

Taiwan
NPLs: 83
% of GDP: 27%
% of total loans: 18%

Mexico**
NPLs: 5
% of GDP: 1%
% of total loans: 7%

Philippines
NPLs: 11
% of GDP: 15%
% of total loans: 38%

Thailand
NPLs: 50
% of GDP: 41%
% of total loans: 45%

Chile**
NPLs: 0.8
% of GDP: 1%
% of total loans: 2%

Argentina**
NPLs: 10
% of GDP: 4%
% of total loans: 12%

Malaysia
NPLs: 43
% of GDP: 48%
% of total loans: 39%

Indonesia
NPLs: 22
% of GDP: 14%
% of total loans: 78%

Your solution

83

Simpler is better

Whereas I find the use of the world map attractive, I don't
have to convince you that this chart has a major legibility
problem. Also, it bothers me that the label for Hungary
is all the way to the left, above those for Mexico and Chile,
when it should be with its geographical colleagues of
Poland and Russia across the top.

Beyond that, I find the repetition of the labels for the three
measures redundant. And it takes up a lot of real estate.

In this case my solution to the problem is to "table it."
By putting all the data in a simple table, I can reduce the
redundant labels, and make the chart legible. Also, the
map is greatly simplified and the table of countries lines
up vertically with their relative positions on the map.
Depending upon the audience, the map could be arranged
with Europe or the U.S. first instead of Asia, as shown.

PROBLEMATIC LOANS ARE A GLOBAL CONCERN
U.S. $ Billions

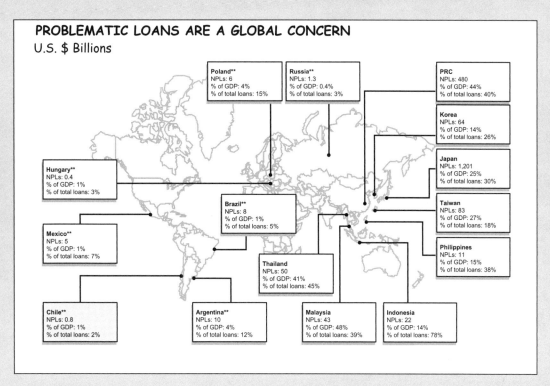

Poland**
NPLs: 6
% of GDP: 4%
% of total loans: 15%

Russia**
NPLs: 1.3
% of GDP: 0.4%
% of total loans: 3%

PRC
NPLs: 480
% of GDP: 44%
% of total loans: 40%

Korea
NPLs: 64
% of GDP: 14%
% of total loans: 26%

Hungary**
NPLs: 0.4
% of GDP: 1%
% of total loans: 3%

Japan
NPLs: 1,201
% of GDP: 25%
% of total loans: 30%

Brazil**
NPLs: 8
% of GDP: 1%
% of total loans: 5%

Taiwan
NPLs: 83
% of GDP: 27%
% of total loans: 18%

Mexico**
NPLs: 5
% of GDP: 1%
% of total loans: 7%

Philippines
NPLs: 11
% of GDP: 15%
% of total loans: 38%

Thailand
NPLs: 50
% of GDP: 41%
% of total loans: 45%

Chile**
NPLs: 0.8
% of GDP: 1%
% of total loans: 2%

Argentina**
NPLs: 10
% of GDP: 4%
% of total loans: 12%

Malaysia
NPLs: 43
% of GDP: 48%
% of total loans: 39%

Indonesia
NPLs: 22
% of GDP: 14%
% of total loans: 78%

PROBLEMATIC LOANS ARE A GLOBAL CONCERN
U.S. $ Billions

	Thailand	Malaysia	Indonesia	PRC	Korea	Japan	Taiwan	Philippines	Mexico	Chile	Argentina	Brazil	Poland	Russia	Hungary
NPLs	50	43	22	480	64	1,201	83	11	5	0.8	10	8	6	1.3	0.4
% of GDP	41	48	14	44	14	25	27	15	1	1	4	1	4	0.4	1
% of total loans	45	39	78	40	26	30	18	38	7	2	12	5	15	3	3

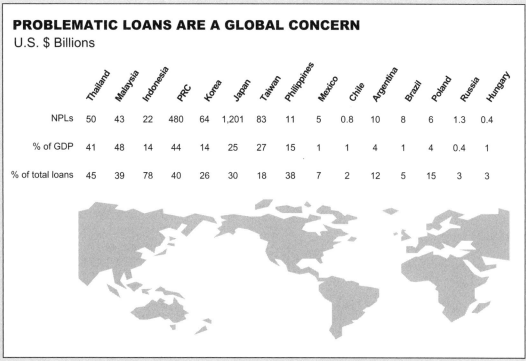

Gene's solution

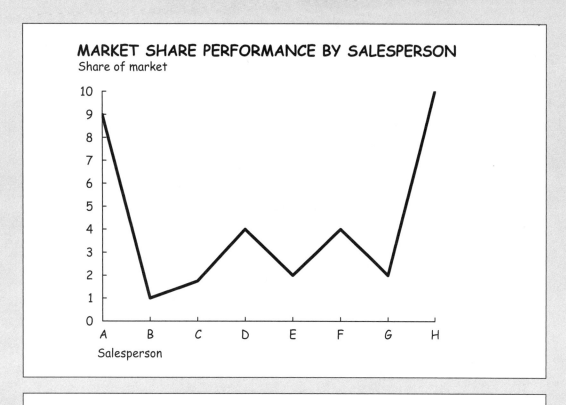

MARKET SHARE PERFORMANCE BY SALESPERSON

Share of market

Salesperson

Your solution

Different is better

This is an example that demonstrates one of the first rules of chart design—that charts provide a quick visual impression and that the title, scale, and footnotes are all secondary to that impression.

When I first looked at this chart, my quick impression was that the share of market went through some wild fluctuations over time, but finally reversed the grave loss it endured in the first period.

When I looked more closely, I realized that this is not a "time series comparison" but an "item comparison" that contrasts the performance of several salespeople. Notice how much faster and more accurate the visual impression becomes when treated as a bar chart.

MARKET SHARE PERFORMANCE BY SALESPERSON

Share of market

Salesperson

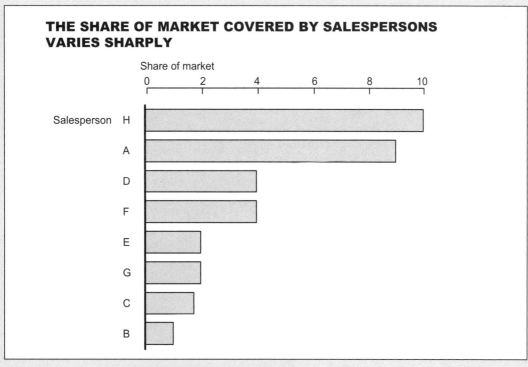

THE SHARE OF MARKET COVERED BY SALESPERSONS VARIES SHARPLY

Share of market

Salesperson

Gene's solution

COMPANY B OUTPERFORMED COMPANY A IN SPITE OF COMPANY A'S GREATER GROWTH IN EMPLOYMENT, ASSETS, AND SALES

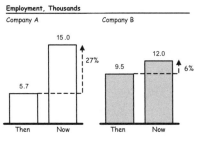

Employment, Thousands

Company A — Then 5.7, Now 15.0, 27%

Company B — Then 9.5, Now 12.0, 6%

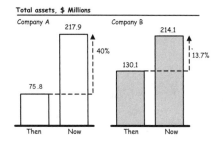

Total assets, $ Millions

Company A — Then 75.8, Now 217.9, 40%

Company B — Then 130.1, Now 214.1, 13.7%

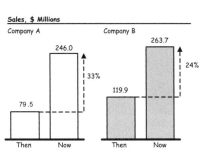

Sales, $ Millions

Company A — Then 79.5, Now 246.0, 33%

Company B — Then 119.9, Now 263.7, 24%

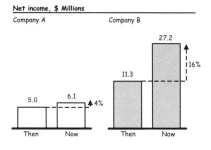

Net income, $ Millions

Company A — Then 5.0, Now 6.1, 4%

Company B — Then 11.3, Now 27.2, 16%

Your solution

Different is better

At times, in our effort to show all the data we've gathered, we plot the wrong figures. Here it's not so much the comparisons of the actual employment, assets, sales, and net income that tells the story, but their percentage change over time—in this case, the average annual growth rates.

By plotting these growth rates, we more clearly and quickly see the reverse pattern mentioned in the message title.

By the way, if showing the absolute values remains important, it's perfectly appropriate to include them in tabular form underneath their respective time periods as you see here at the bottom of the chart.

COMPANY B OUTPERFORMED COMPANY A IN SPITE OF COMPANY A'S GREATER GROWTH IN EMPLOYMENT, ASSETS, AND SALES

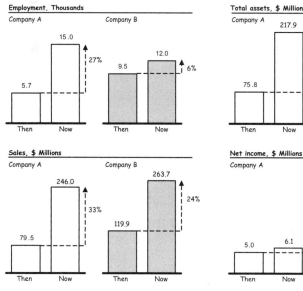

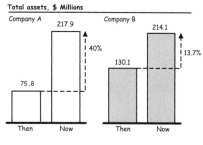

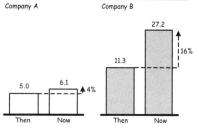

IN SPITE OF COMPANY A'S GREATER GROWTH IN SALES, ASSETS AND EMPLOYMENT, COMPANY B OUTPERFORMED COMPANY A

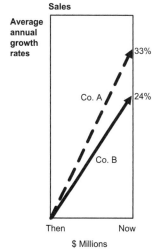

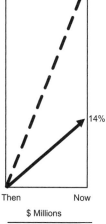

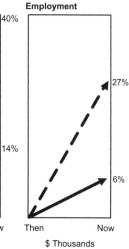

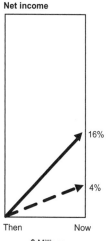

	Sales		Assets		Employment		Net income	
	Then	Now	Then	Now	Then	Now	Then	Now
	$ Millions		$ Millions		$ Thousands		$ Millions	
Co. A	79.5	246.0	75.8	27.9	5.7	15.0	5.0	6.1
Co. B	119.9	263.7	130.4	214.1	9.5	12.0	11.3	27.2

Gene's solution   93

EXTERNAL RESEARCH SUPPLIERS ARE USED HEAVILY IN ALL AREAS OF RESEARCH

■ External research department
□ Internal research department

Relative frequency of use of inside versus external research

Advertising research

100%

33	52	51
67	48	49

Copy research | Media research | Ad effectiveness

Product research

100%

74	86	88
26	14	12

Packaging design | Product testing | New product acceptance

Sales & market research

100%

63	74	62	84	55	54
37	26	38	16	45	46

Consumer panels | Store audits | Promotions | Market share analysis | Channel studies | Sales quotas

Your solution

Different is better

I work very hard to make sure that I don't ask the reader
to turn his or her head in order to read the labels at
the bottom of each column, as you must here. Similarly,
I work hard to avoid forcing the reader to look back and
forth between the legend and the chart itself to see what
corresponds to what.

Here, by using horizontal bars instead of vertical columns,
more room is allowed for the labels, so they may be read
normally. Also, we can delete the legend and make its
information part of the chart. We do this with a sliding
100 percent bar chart, using the line that separates internal
and external as the base line so the differences between
them are more clearly contrasted.

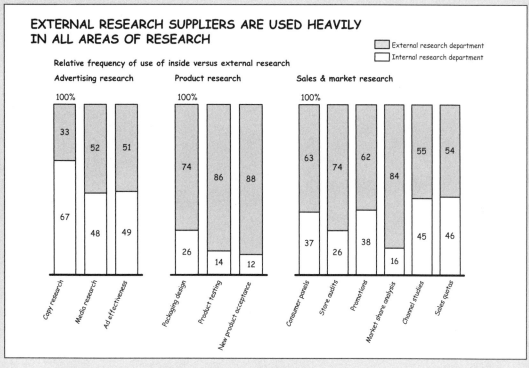

EXTERNAL RESEARCH SUPPLIERS ARE USED HEAVILY IN ALL AREAS OF RESEARCH

■ External research department
□ Internal research department

Relative frequency of use of inside versus external research

Advertising research | Product research | Sales & market research

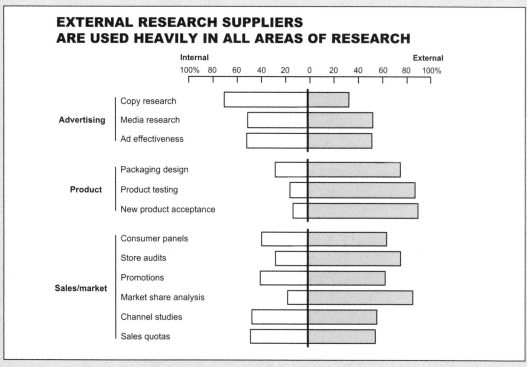

EXTERNAL RESEARCH SUPPLIERS
ARE USED HEAVILY IN ALL AREAS OF RESEARCH

Gene's solution

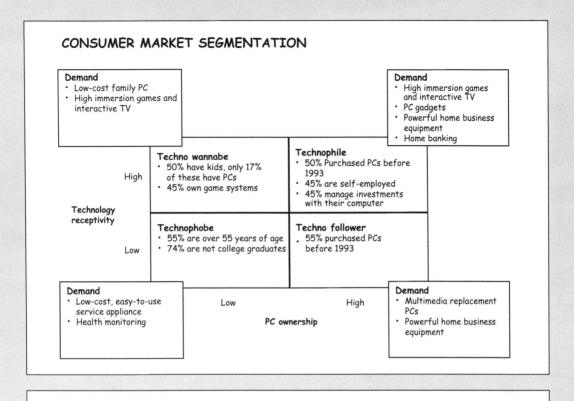

CONSUMER MARKET SEGMENTATION

Demand
- Low-cost family PC
- High immersion games and interactive TV

Demand
- High immersion games and interactive TV
- PC gadgets
- Powerful home business equipment
- Home banking

Techno wannabe
- 50% have kids, only 17% of these have PCs
- 45% own game systems

Technophile
- 50% Purchased PCs before 1993
- 45% are self-employed
- 45% manage investments with their computer

High

Technology receptivity

Low

Technophobe
- 55% are over 55 years of age
- 74% are not college graduates

Techno follower
- 55% purchased PCs before 1993

Demand
- Low-cost, easy-to-use service appliance
- Health monitoring

Low   High

PC ownership

Demand
- Multimedia replacement PCs
- Powerful home business equipment

Your solution

Creativity is better

As is, the chart does a good job of presenting the characteristics and demand for four segments of the consumer market for technology. It would be fine to leave it that way for the handout.

If you were doing an onscreen presentation, however, a "More is better" solution would be to design several visuals: the first to introduce the four quadrants, the second through fifth, to show the detailed characteristics and demand for each of the four quadrants.

My real-life situation in dealing with this material involved a large audience at an off-site conference. So we took the challenge one step further. As you see, we characterized the four quadrants with illustrations that gave a personality to each segment, leaving the speaker free to elaborate in as much or as little detail as the audience needed.

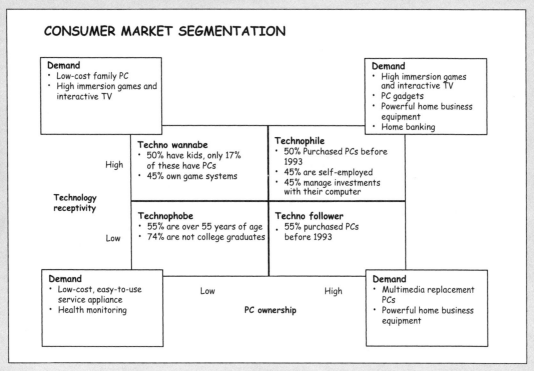

CONSUMER MARKET SEGMENTATION

Demand
- Low-cost family PC
- High immersion games and interactive TV

Demand
- High immersion games and interactive TV
- PC gadgets
- Powerful home business equipment
- Home banking

Technology receptivity

High

Techno wannabe
- 50% have kids, only 17% of these have PCs
- 45% own game systems

Technophile
- 50% Purchased PCs before 1993
- 45% are self-employed
- 45% manage investments with their computer

Low

Technophobe
- 55% are over 55 years of age
- 74% are not college graduates

Techno follower
- 55% purchased PCs before 1993

Demand
- Low-cost, easy-to-use service appliance
- Health monitoring

Low   High

PC ownership

Demand
- Multimedia replacement PCs
- Powerful home business equipment

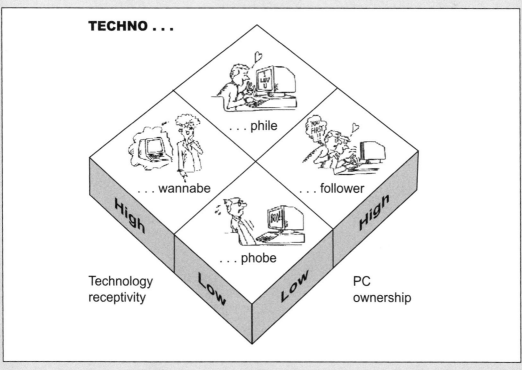

TECHNO . . .

. . . phile

. . . wannabe

. . . follower

. . . phobe

High

Low   Low

High

Technology receptivity

PC ownership

Gene's solution

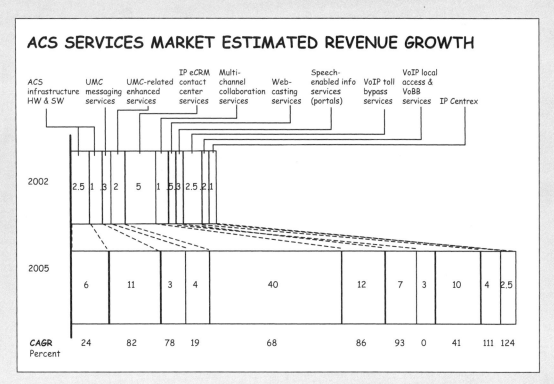

ACS SERVICES MARKET ESTIMATED REVENUE GROWTH

	ACS infrastructure HW & SW	UMC messaging services	UMC-related enhanced services	IP eCRM contact center services	Multi-channel collaboration services	Web-casting services	Speech-enabled info services (portals)	VoIP toll bypass services	VoIP local access & VoBB services	IP Centrex
2002	2.5 1 .3 2		5	1 .5 .3	2.5 .2 .1					
2005	6	11	3	4	40		12	7	3	10 4 2.5
CAGR Percent	24	82	78	19	68		86	93	0	41 111 124

Your solution

HOLD  N!

Earn
extra
CREDIT

Think of **ANOTHER WAY**

Different is (mercifully) better

Let's nominate this one to the charting Hall of Shame.
It's both illegible and too complex. It took me some time,
but I've come up with two possible solutions.

1. Multiple column charts show the pattern over time for
    each of the components. Respective growth is much
    more apparent because everything is measured against
    a common base. *(I left off the CAGRs—compound annual
    growth rates—but I could have included them to the right of
    the second column.)*

2. As I show on the back of the facing page, sometimes it's
    simpler to leave information in tabular form. I realize
    that I've already said that tabular data merely implies
    comparisons whereas charts demonstrate them.
    However, a table works better here because the numbers
    line up with each other, making the comparison easy.
    If nothing else, it certainly works many times better than
    the original treatment.

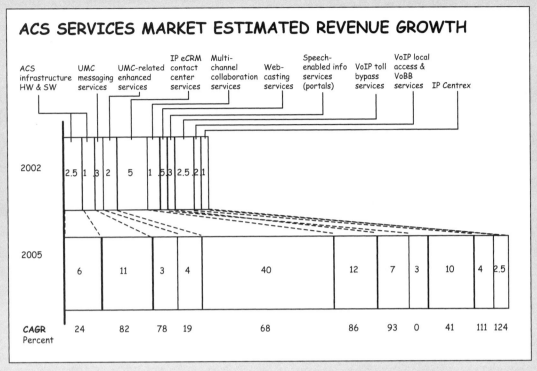

ACS SERVICES MARKET ESTIMATED REVENUE GROWTH

	ACS infrastructure HW & SW	UMC messaging services	UMC-related enhanced services	IP eCRM contact center services	Multi-channel collaboration services	Web-casting services	Speech-enabled info services (portals)	VoIP toll bypass services	VoIP local access & VoBB services	IP Centrex
2002	2.5	1	3	2	5	1	5 3	2.5 2	1	
2005	6	11	3	4	40		12	7	3	10	4	2.5
CAGR Percent	24	82	78	19	68		86	93	0	41	111	124

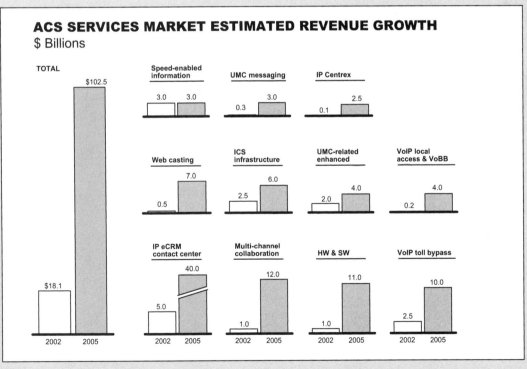

ACS SERVICES MARKET ESTIMATED REVENUE GROWTH
$ Billions

TOTAL
- 2002: $18.1
- 2005: $102.5

Speed-enabled information
- 3.0 / 3.0

UMC messaging
- 0.3 / 3.0

IP Centrex
- 0.1 / 2.5

Web casting
- 0.5 / 7.0

ICS infrastructure
- 2.5 / 6.0

UMC-related enhanced
- 2.0 / 4.0

VoIP local access & VoBB
- 0.2 / 4.0

IP eCRM contact center
- 5.0 / 40.0

Multi-channel collaboration
- 1.0 / 12.0

HW & SW
- 1.0 / 11.0

VoIP toll bypass
- 2.5 / 10.0

Gene's solution No. 1

ACS SERVICES MARKET ESTIMATED REVENUE GROWTH

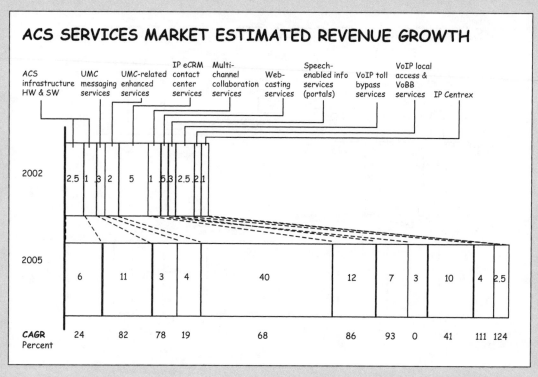

ACS SERVICES MARKET ESTIMATED REVENUE GROWTH
$ Billions

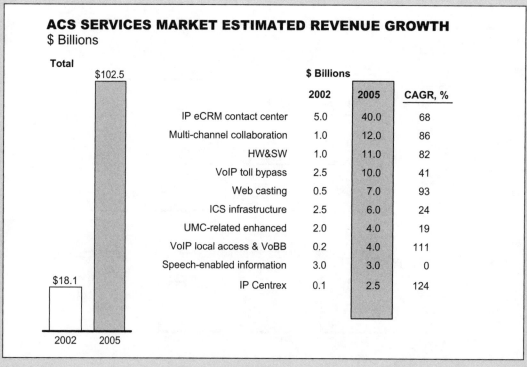

	2002	2005	CAGR, %
IP eCRM contact center	5.0	40.0	68
Multi-channel collaboration	1.0	12.0	86
HW&SW	1.0	11.0	82
VoIP toll bypass	2.5	10.0	41
Web casting	0.5	7.0	93
ICS infrastructure	2.5	6.0	24
UMC-related enhanced	2.0	4.0	19
VoIP local access & VoBB	0.2	4.0	111
Speech-enabled information	3.0	3.0	0
IP Centrex	0.1	2.5	124

Total: $102.5 (2005), $18.1 (2002)

Gene's solution No. 2

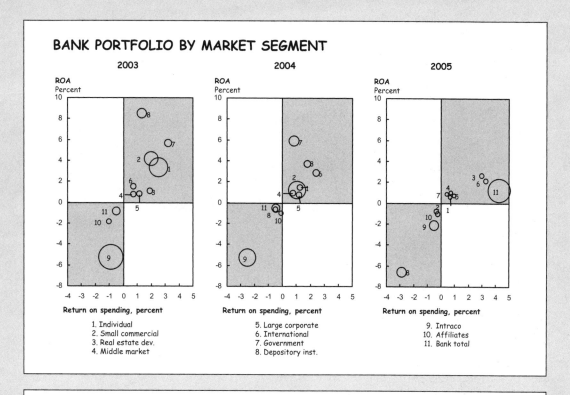

BANK PORTFOLIO BY MARKET SEGMENT

2003   **2004**   **2005**

1. Individual
2. Small commercial
3. Real estate dev.
4. Middle market
5. Large corporate
6. International
7. Government
8. Depository inst.
9. Intraco
10. Affiliates
11. Bank total

Your solution

More and different are better

Give up? How much effort did it take you to follow the
bouncing numbers ... and their changing sizes ... over the
three time horizons ... to figure out the message of this chart?

As you can see from my solution, one answer is to divide
the message into its component thoughts and use five
separate slides to get the story across. I've shown them all
on one visual here, which would work for a handout. For
an onscreen presentation to a large audience, you may want
to show the first two in one slide as you explain how to read
the upcoming charts, then show the next three, full-screen,
in succession to ensure legibility.

The first two visuals explain the axes of the matrix and how
to read the chart. The latter three show the pattern for the
segments that became more profitable, those that showed
no change, and those that lost their position over the three
years.

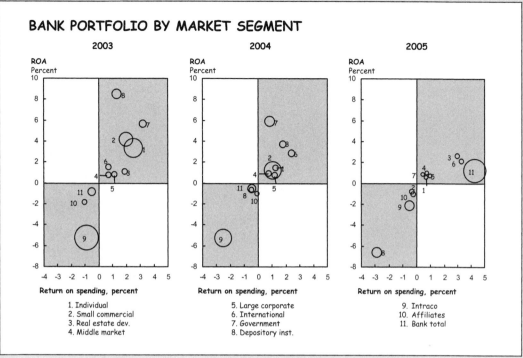

BANK PORTFOLIO BY MARKET SEGMENT

2003

ROA
Percent

Return on spending, percent

2004

ROA
Percent

Return on spending, percent

2005

ROA
Percent

Return on spending, percent

1. Individual
2. Small commercial
3. Real estate dev.
4. Middle market

5. Large corporate
6. International
7. Government
8. Depository inst.

9. Intraco
10. Affiliates
11. Bank total

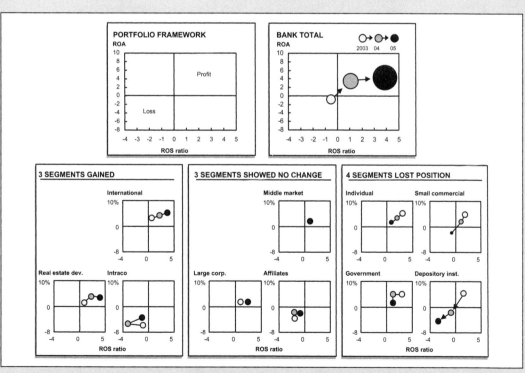

PORTFOLIO FRAMEWORK
ROA
Profit
Loss
ROS ratio

BANK TOTAL
ROA
2003   04   05
ROS ratio

3 SEGMENTS GAINED
International
Real estate dev.   Intraco
ROS ratio

3 SEGMENTS SHOWED NO CHANGE
Middle market
Large corp.   Affiliates
ROS ratio

4 SEGMENTS LOST POSITION
Individual   Small commercial
Government   Depository inst.
ROS ratio

Gene's solution

111

GETTING THE BASICS RIGHT FOR PUBLIC SCHOOL

- Develop, attract, and retain excellent principals and teachers

- Improve school curricula, academic programs, and learning environments

- Develop a customer service-oriented central administration that excels at support to schools

- Maximize the dollars used to improve student achievement

- Enable and energize parent and community involvement

- Optimize interagency coordination

Your solution

Creativity is better

I include this last one only to remind you that, at times, your best bet for finding ways to develop creative and interesting visuals is to look in the fourth edition of my book, *Say It with Charts*. Just turn to Section 3, and the chapter I subtitle "Solutions in Search of Problems." This chapter offers a range of ideas for concept visuals.

Here is a sampling of the options I found.

GETTING THE BASICS RIGHT FOR PUBLIC SCHOOL

- Develop, attract, and retain excellent principals and teachers

- Improve school curricula, academic programs, and learning environments

- Develop a customer service-oriented central administration that excels at support to schools

- Maximize the dollars used to improve student achievement

- Enable and energize parent and community involvement

- Optimize interagency coordination

GETTING THE BASICS RIGHT FOR PUBLIC SCHOOL

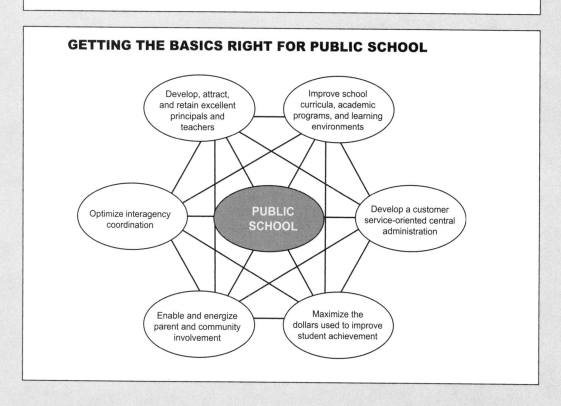

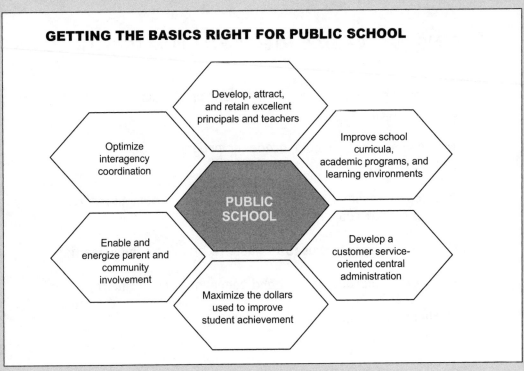

GETTING THE BASICS RIGHT FOR PUBLIC SCHOOL

Develop, attract, and retain excellent principals and teachers

Optimize interagency coordination

Improve school curricula, academic programs, and learning environments

PUBLIC SCHOOL

Enable and energize parent and community involvement

Develop a customer service-oriented central administration

Maximize the dollars used to improve student achievement

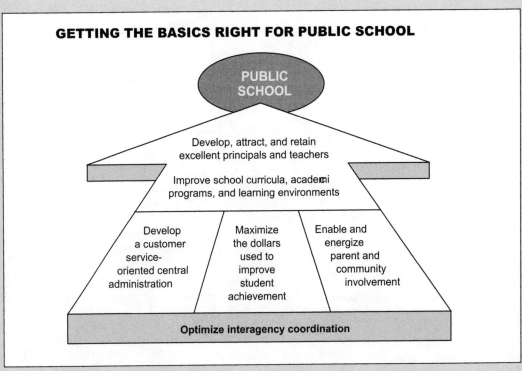

GETTING THE BASICS RIGHT FOR PUBLIC SCHOOL

PUBLIC SCHOOL

Develop, attract, and retain excellent principals and teachers

Improve school curricula, academic programs, and learning environments

Develop a customer service-oriented central administration

Maximize the dollars used to improve student achievement

Enable and energize parent and community involvement

Optimize interagency coordination

116

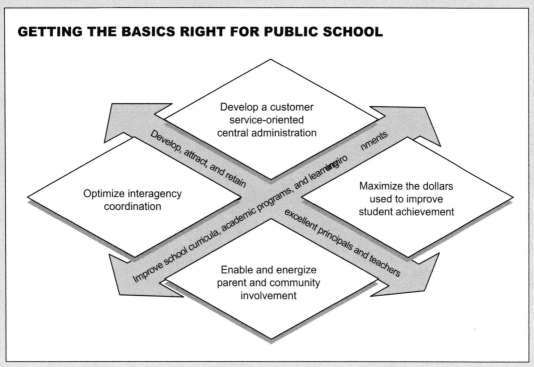

GETTING THE BASICS RIGHT FOR PUBLIC SCHOOL

Develop a customer service-oriented central administration

Develop, attract, and retain

Improve school curricula, academic programs, and learning enviro nments

excellent principals and teachers

Optimize interagency coordination

Maximize the dollars used to improve student achievement

Enable and energize parent and community involvement

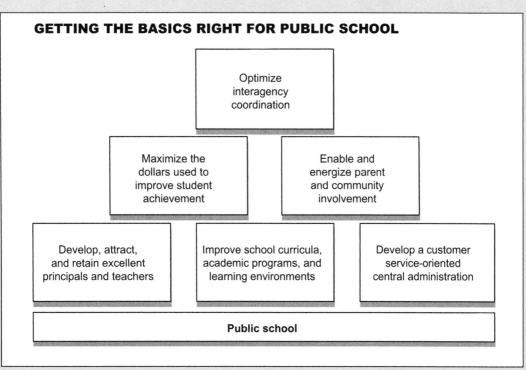

GETTING THE BASICS RIGHT FOR PUBLIC SCHOOL

Optimize interagency coordination

Maximize the dollars used to improve student achievement

Enable and energize parent and community involvement

Develop, attract, and retain excellent principals and teachers

Improve school curricula, academic programs, and learning environments

Develop a customer service-oriented central administration

Public school

GETTING THE BASICS RIGHT FOR PUBLIC SCHOOL

Develop, attract, and retain excellent principals and teachers	Improve school curricula, academic programs, and learning environments	Develop a customer service-oriented central administration
Maximize the dollars used to improve student achievement	Enable and energize parent and community involvement	Optimize interagency coordination

GETTING THE BASICS RIGHT FOR PUBLIC SCHOOL

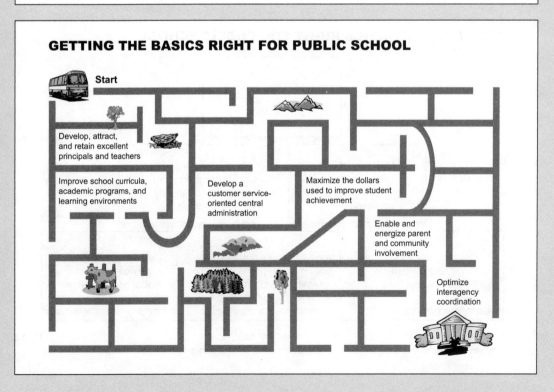

118

GETTING THE BASICS RIGHT FOR PUBLIC SCHOOL

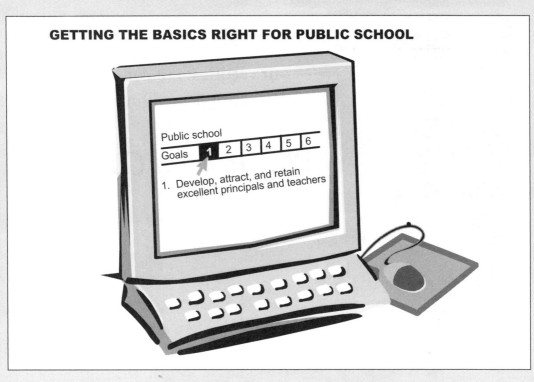

GETTING THE BASICS RIGHT FOR PUBLIC SCHOOL

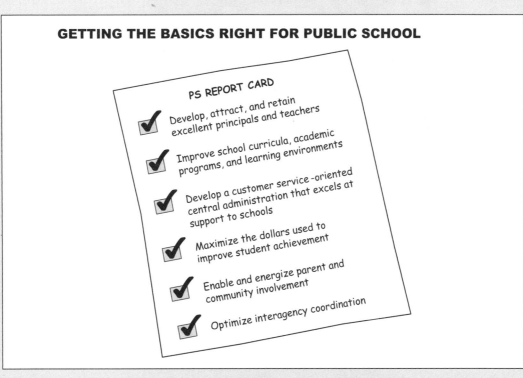

119

Congratulations!

Here's your certificate of completion
for your willingness to

Play It With Charts

Index

ABOUT GENE ZELAZNY

Gene Zelazny is the Director of Visual Communications for McKinsey & Company.

His primary responsibility has been to provide creative advice and assistance to the professional staff in the design of visual presentations and written reports. This includes planning the communication strategy; structuring the story line; interpreting the data or concepts and recommending the best visual formats in terms of charts, diagrams, etc.; designing storyboards; and rehearsing the delivery of the presentation. He is also responsible for designing and conducting communication training programs.

Gene regularly presents his ideas in a talk called "Making the Most of Your Business Presentation," which he has delivered at such business schools as Chicago, Columbia, Cornell, Darden, Harvard, Haas, Kellogg, Illinois, Michigan, Sloan, Stanford, Tuck, UCLA, Wharton, and Washington, in the U.S., and INSEAD, LBS, and Oxford in Europe.

His first book, *Say It with Charts*, was first published in 1985, and is now available in six languages. The sequel, *Say It with Presentations*, was published in 2000. Upcoming is his newest book, *Say It with Imagination*, in which he will describe ways you can combine creativity with today's multimedia tools to impress and inspire audiences to action.

On a personal basis, you can see Gene having fun playing tennis, riding his bicycle, designing original chess sets (check out his Web site, **www.zelazny.com**), toying with his grandson, all while holding hands with Judy. His book of personal essays, *In the Moment*, is available on **www.amazon.com**.

124